AUDACIOUS
DESTRUCTION

Why a two-term Obama presidency will destroy the Rule of Law and your wallet

GEORGE BALL

DEDICATION

To my loving wife Dianne for her support in this multi-year research and writing effort and for her constant reminders, as a life-long educator, to scrap the legalese and write for the broadest possible audience instead of just lawyers and academics. And for Colonel William (Bill) Kelly, U.S. Army (ret), who recently passed away after a year-long battle with pancreatic cancer, for being the best friend a person could have and for his painstaking review of the early drafts of this book.

CONTENTS

INTRODUCTION

This book is for anyone who wants to dig deeper than the daily chatter from talking heads in the media to find the root cause of our economy's stagnation and the *uncertainty* that permeates our business and personal financial decisions. Whether you are in your '20s or '70s, work in a factory or the front office, and regardless of your race, you know down deep that something is fundamentally wrong with our great country. You can't sell your home; you have lost your job; your retirement savings are in a shambles; your church leaders are being dictated to by the president and Washington bureaucrats; your children and grandchildren are being forced to pay for the debts of our spendthrift politicians; your taxes are going up and your personal freedoms are going down because the government has decided to redistribute your hard earned income and give it to someone else. Why did we descend to these depths and what do we have to do to right this great ship called America?

When we look beyond the hyperbole of self-interested politicians and the so-called experts, what we discover is that the fabric of our democratic society is torn and in desperate need of repair. The Rule of Law, which has been around since Aristotle's time in classical Greece, is the foundation of the personal freedoms and economic success we take for granted in the United States. But after decades of mistreatment, the Rule of Law is on life support.

If there is any hope of resuscitating this national treasure and returning our country to economic growth and the vibrancy that comes from expanded personal freedom, there is only one question we should all be asking: Will a two-term Obama presidency destroy the Rule of Law and your bank account? In this book, I will answer that question in the unvarnished, direct way I would give advice to a client - without legal jargon.

As a young attorney I was on the front lines at General Motors in Detroit when the tsunami of emissions, safety and fuel economy statutes and regulations struck GM in the early to mid-1970s and the traditional or formal understanding of the Rule of Law took some real hits. I was the head of the product regulation department on the General Motors legal staff in the late 1980s and early 1990s when the misguided fuel economy mandates, in particular, were in full swing and their long term damage to GM and the consumer was becoming evident.

As the General Counsel at Suzuki in the 1990s and as Suzuki's point man in its epic eight-year product disparagement battle against *Consumer Reports* magazine that ended in 2004, I led Suzuki's efforts to stand up for its rule of law rights around the country. We fended off frivolous lawsuits involving the Suzuki Samurai sport utility vehicle and fought to restore its reputation in our litigation with *Consumer Reports*. From those experiences, it became perfectly clear to me how some judges, who are supposed to be impartial under the Rule of Law, could sway a case away from the facts and law toward their personal preferences.

So when President Barack Obama (Obama) began his assault on the Rule of Law with a wealth redistributionist legislative agenda, a flurry of ideologically driven regulatory actions by his political appointee bureaucrats and his efforts to reshape the courts with like-minded rule of law challenged judges, I had seen much of it before. I decided to write this book to expose the tragic abuse of the rule of law because most politicians were not going to rescue this great ideal. If the Rule of Law were going to get new life, it would have to come from the bottom up.

I have spent my career giving straightforward advice so that a non-lawyer client can understand it and act on the advice. That is how I've written this book. Hopefully, it will help us all understand how important the Rule of Law is to our daily lives and the penalty we all pay when this ideal is trampled upon. If so, then I will have done my small part in trying to move this country on to better days.

As I have said, the rule of law ideal that holds in a free society - where we answer only to the law and not to the will of men - is on life support today. So what difference does it make to "John Q. Public" - whether he or she is a factory worker, software engineer, retired army officer, or CEO - that politicians and judges make light of this unwritten political ideal? The answer, and the reason I wrote this book, is that its continued denigration has the potential to alter our lives and put us on the "road to serfdom" in the words of the renowned economist and philosopher, F.A. Hayek, if this course is not reversed. We need to be constantly reminded that there is a difference between "legality" and meeting the Rule of Law. For example, authoritarian regimes may be elected and be "legal" but laws they pass persecuting minorities or expropriating assets from one class and giving them to another, do not meet the Rule of Law.

Since this nation's founding, the formal rule of law ideal in the U.S. can be summed up in a few succinct principles: That laws are supreme and apply to rulers and the ruled alike; and as a safeguard to protect the ideal, all laws and lawmakers should meet constitutional safeguards at a minimum; that laws should be passed by lawmakers following long-established legal principles and voting procedures and that laws should have the stabilizing attributes of "generality," "certainty" and "equality" of application to all. And to ensure that properly enacted laws will not be nullified when applied to individuals in the real world, they should be enforced by government officials fully and impartially and judges should act in a dispassionate and objective manner when interpreting and applying the laws to parties in court. And for most of our history judges did so.

Political theorists have concluded that laws with these attributes best protect the personal freedoms and economic well being of all citizens. Since the laws were supposed to apply equally to all and legislators or lawmakers did not take from one class and give their wealth to another, it could be said that laws, not men, were supreme.

To most Americans, though, the rule of law ideal is an abstraction that is hard to define. But if asked, most people would probably have a vague sense that it means something like, under American law everyone gets an equal shot at personal and economic freedom and that some government official cannot take that away from you without complying with the laws on the books and a fair hearing in court. Well that is close and in the chapters that follow, it will be defined in more detail.

For introductory purposes, though, having played hockey in high school and college, a sports analogy comes to mind. We go to see professional sports teams play a sport because we appreciate the players' skills that result from natural talent, discipline and hard work. But we keep buying tickets and returning to the sports arenas because we trust that the rules of the game are not skewed toward any one team or player and that the referees will apply them objectively to everyone. Consequently, the Super Bowl is watched by more people in the U.S. than virtually any other event. Just as sports fans would shout their disapproval at a sporting event if they thought the referees were throwing the game to one team over another and eventually stop buying tickets, in the great game of American political and economic life, we are approaching that point.

As our economy has soured with mercilessly high gas prices, $15 trillion in debt and counting, millions unemployed and home prices that are so low sellers have to reach up to touch bottom, many are losing faith and confidence in the U.S. and are voicing their discontent. And whether the public realizes it or not, the root cause of this discontent can be laid at the doorstep of many of our government officials. They have a history of picking partisan favorites - thus taking us all down - by distorting the rules of the game or, in other words, the Rule of Law. To put it bluntly, as we move into the second decade of the 21st century, decades of laws, administrative regulations and judicial decisions - that have been cobbled up to accomplish special interest objectives - are catching up with us. The acceleration of the effort to weaken the Rule of Law ideal during the Obama administration has resulted in a disturbing loss of consumer and business confidence in the American economy. Just as attendance and ticket revenue would fall off dramatically if Super Bowl rules were adulterated, as the Rule of Law becomes more of a slogan than a reality in the U.S., Americans and many of our foreign cousins are losing their appetite for investing their effort or money in our historically great country.

But among his predecessors, who also played fast and loose with the Rule of Law - Franklin D. Roosevelt and Richard Nixon to name just two - President Obama stands above the rest in his capability to tip the rule of law ideal over the edge. He has the power and inclination to alter irreparably this country's traditional legal system and the free enterprise economy that depends on the Rule of Law for its foundation. He alone is a former law professor who was educated and indoctrinated by left-leaning and radical professors - with agendas that were impacted and stimulated by the anti-establishment protest era of the 1960s. Of the many professors who Obama interacted with at the Harvard Law School two stand out in particular: one, a liberal sycophantic constitutional law professor and the other a self-proclaimed revolutionary who taught Obama how to undermine traditional legal principles. This background when linked to his populist message and beguiling manner has captivated many trusting, naturally gullible Americans. If Franklin Roosevelt or Richard Nixon were alive today they would be no match for President Obama's potential to emasculate what's left of the rule of law ideal.

Like poorly designed nuclear power plants, our legal and economic systems are suffering a fallout from this onslaught. In addition to an employment rate hovering around 8% and a home foreclosure catastrophe, we have an immigration law nightmare, a healthcare system in disarray and a struggling consumer credit industry under the thumb of a virtually unaccountable bureaucrat. Obama Care (The Patient Protection and Affordable Care Act) and the Dodd-Frank financial system legislation (Wall Street Reform and Consumer Protection Act) are just two examples of actions taken during President Obama's first term that weakened our country's rule of law ideal. And contrary to the Rule of Law, Obama Care is still standing today because the Supreme Court's Chief Justice, John Roberts, obviously blinked in the game of chicken with the Obama administration and caved into its Supreme Court intimidation efforts. There is little question that he violated the separation of powers principle of the Rule of Law and appointed himself a congressman in his June 28, 2012 opinion upholding the "individual mandate" under the law. In effect, he rewrote Obama's law so that failure to meet the individual mandate to buy health insurance became a permissible 'tax" instead of an unconstitutional "penalty" under Obama Care. Adding insult to injury, in his quest to rewrite the law, Chief Justice Roberts also ignored the fact that Congress and President Obama led America to believe it was not a *tax* to help get enough votes to ram the health care bill through Congress.

And Obama Care is not alone in its constitutional problems; a lawsuit challenging Dodd-Frank's constitutionality is pending in court. Combine Obama's legislative agenda and the stranglehold that Obama's regulators have over society - with the high likelihood that he may be able to appoint more like-minded Supreme Court justices if re-elected - and the tipping point will be reached. And sadly for all, the death knell will sound for the classic rule of law protections our country and economy are based upon.

American society in the 21st century, with our basic constitutional protections, is much better off than the American colonists in 1776 that were compelled to demand their "rule of law" rights when faced with the tyranny of King George III and Parliament. However, if we are going to avoid traveling down the "road to serfdom" - a road in which the Rule of Law becomes a malleable piece of clay that fits the desired ends of self-serving government officials instead of a firm yardstick that protects all of us - a legal renaissance is imperative.

To overcome the current view of many in the political class and the members of the judiciary who share their view that the Rule of Law is often "impracticable or even undesirable," this ideal will have to become a "part of the moral tradition of the community" to borrow a phrase from Hayek. While we have much work to do in this country to achieve that goal, based on the real life examples set by Margaret Thatcher and Ronald Reagan, there is hope that free enterprise founded on the Rule of Law can and will thrive again. There is little question, though, that if the protections of the Rule of Law and the economic success it produces for all are to be realized in the U.S. in the 21st century, the movement will have to come from "we the people" with a little help from like-minded political and legal community leaders. Remember that most politicians are focused on getting re-elected and to many of them - especially someone as convicted of his ideology and personal preferences as President Obama - the Rule of Law is nothing more than an "impediment" to be avoided.

As the economic and political crises we now face in America attest to, man's law-making fallibility has caught up with us. We have cobbled together one too many laws to satisfy narrow special interests and judges have decided one too many cases with an eye on personal preferences rather than discovering and applying the law as it stands. Hopefully the chapters that follow will provide insight into the importance of the Rule of Law in our daily lives and the need to insist on its fulfillment by all government officials so as to get this country back on a much-needed successful course.

CHAPTER 1

Indoctrination at Harvard and the Sycophantic Professor

It has been said that at the Harvard Law School an "ACLU liberal is considered a centrist."[1] And the Harvard Law School professors who would have a profound impact on law student Barack Obama's view of the Rule of Law during his student days in Cambridge-1988-91-were true to form; one, a liberal sycophantic constitutional law professor and the other a self-proclaimed revolutionary who taught Obama how to undermine traditional legal principles.

So when first-year Harvard law student Barack Obama visited the office of the outspoken, liberal constitutional law professor, Laurence Tribe, in March 1989, he was right in step with the campus's prevailing ideology. As the story goes, he ostensibly stopped by to discuss Tribe's academic writings.[2] This would be the beginning of a relationship with Obama in which Tribe fawned over his politically ambitious student. And it would eventually include Tribe campaigning for Obama when he ran for the presidency in 2008 and to Obama even finding a place for Tribe in his administration, as we shall see later in this book.[3] Tribe's unusual mentor relationship with Obama, which could not help but shape the impressionable Barack Obama's view of constitutional law and the role of judges and lawyers in the legal process, began when Tribe asked Obama to be one of his research assistants.[4]

As incredible as it sounds to me - as a lawyer who has spent 40 years in practice - Tribe was hesitant to ask Obama to do the nuts and bolts work that law students should do to appreciate the importance of *stare decisis* or, in other words, the reliance on precedent. *Stare decisis* is a key foundational principle of American law and it helps young lawyers realize the humble place we lawyers fit into the long and rule of law inspired history of our profession. Tribe would later indicate in an interview, "I didn't think of him as someone to send out on the mechanical tasks of digging out all the cases." Instead, Tribe saw Obama more as a "colleague" and the two of them would take strolls along the Charles River and exchange lofty ideas about law and society.[5]

What makes this Tribe-Obama relationship a little hard to explain is that it was not based on evidence of Obama's extraordinary academic performance in undergraduate school leading up to his admission to Harvard. Obama graduated from Columbia University in 1983 with a major in political science. His academic performance at Columbia was considered "unspectacular."[6] And "some of his Harvard friends said that Obama believed affirmative action had likely helped get him into Columbia and Harvard."[7] Confirming the comments of his friends, Obama admitted in a letter written during his Harvard Law School days that he "undoubtedly benefitted from affirmative action programs during [his] academic career...."[8] So for all those who were willing to suspend your disbelief in 2008 and accept the media myth that Obama was somehow intellectually "supernatural" and that he is above the Rule of Law that applies to everyone else, think again. Instead of some innate wisdom that would make Mensa society members look like intellectually challenged poor cousins, he has simply used the "tools" and Harvard bestowed halo to "undermine" this country's legal DNA - the Rule of Law - and thereby pervert, instead of preserve, the Constitution.

In his memoirs, *Dreams From My Father* and *Audacity of Hope*, Obama virtually ignores his experience at the elite institutions he attended and thereby shielded from in-depth scrutiny his "unspectacular" academic performance and the left-leaning nature of his undergraduate and law school education. As would be evident later, as more of his history became public after his 2008 campaign, many of his undergraduate professors were involved in the 1960s movements and "regaled students" with stories from those years.[9] Obama's professors were replacing the World War II generation of educators, "the greatest generation" in Tom Brokaw's words, and were passing on to their students the values of the Vietnam era protest movements.[10]

Probably the most likely conclusion one can draw from the Tribe mentor relationship with Obama is that Tribe let his liberal giddiness take over for the mature leadership and good judgment that a senior educator should demonstrate toward a first-year law student. "Over the years Obama stayed in touch with Tribe and Minow (another liberal Harvard law professor and dean) and discussed electronic eavesdropping, Guantanamo… [and] future Supreme Court justices." On occasion they disagreed with Tribe even getting to the left of Obama, for example, about "same-sex marriages … which Tribe supported and Obama [originally] opposed."[11]

Applying Tribe's views to the role of judges in our legal system, Obama would have been schooled in the belief that "judges are compelled to advance contemporary notions of justice."[12] This liberal view of the role of the judiciary obviously plays fast and loose with the rule of law ideal. Judges should be completely objective and dispassionate in their rulings. They should discover the law as set forth in the Constitution, cases and statutes and not "make" law so as to "advance contemporary notions of justice."

Based on my involvement with judges in various trial and appellate courts, Tribe's view, which is unfortunately held by many judges, is often nothing more than a code for inserting one's personal preference into judicial decision-making. One noted legal scholar from the University of Chicago Law School has expressed serious constitutionally based concerns about the Tribe type of judicial interpretation philosophy relative to the "potentially undemocratic character of judicial intrusion into political processes."[13]

Tribe had also become somewhat of a hero among the anti-conservative left-leaning Washington establishment a year before Obama arrived in Cambridge. As the politically astute young law student Obama probably knew, Tribe had been the star witness in the 1987 Supreme Court confirmation hearings for President Reagan's nominee, Robert Bork. In fact, Tribe not only testified at the hearing as a purported objective law school professor critical of Bork's conservative judicial philosophy, but he also played the part of Robert Bork in mock hearings in the living room of the then Senator Joe Biden, chairman of the Senate Judiciary Committee.[14]

Bork, like many conservative judges, was a proponent of the "originalism" school of judicial interpretation of the Constitution, which is anathema to Tribe and his followers. Consistent with the traditional rule of law ideal, it holds that judges should look to the words of the constitution and the framers' original understanding of those words when deciding constitutional questions and not outside the Constitution to so-called "contemporary notions of justice" as Tribe and other liberals advocate. Exposing what many believe to be the real motivation behind the Tribe inspired judicial interpretation philosophy, Bork once observed that "[t]he truth is that the judge who looks outside the constitution always looks inside himself and nowhere else."[15]

From my years of experience preparing for congressional and federal agency hearings and arguments in court, the only reason Biden would conduct mock hearings was so that Biden could sharpen his attack on President Reagan's conservative nominee for the Supreme Court. Among other liberal concerns, Bork did not agree with the so-called constitutional reasoning that supported the controversial 1973 abortion decision, Roe v Wade.[16] The mock hearings in his living room certainly weren't intended to help Biden be a more effective and objective fact-gatherer at Bork's hearing; a more legitimate and rule of law based role for the chairman of such an important Senate committee. For those who don't remember how this chapter in American history ended, Tribe's lengthy testimony in combination with the well-rehearsed Joe Biden hearing and Senator Ted Kennedy's excoriating televised speech on the Senate floor, led to the senate voting against Bork's 1987 nomination. It meant little to the Senate interrogators that Bork was an eminent U.S. federal appellate court jurist and legal scholar at that time.[17] If Obama had been watching these hearings the year before he arrived at Harvard, he would have seen how important Tribe's testimony and academic credentials had been in giving an academic and legal system "cover" to Biden and Kennedy for their ideological attacks. Naturally this is someone who the aspiring liberal politician would want to seek out as a mentor at Harvard. The historical significance of the Bork episode is palpable when one considers that Kennedy would break ranks with the Clintons and endorse Obama during the 2008 campaign season and Biden would later become Obama's vice president.[18]

Combine Tribe's ideologically based views of the law with student Obama's charm and his life narrative and you have the ingredients for their liberal professor-student marriage made in heaven relationship. As a former General Counsel who has interviewed, worked with and managed hundreds of lawyers and law students in my career - many from the so-called elite law schools - I know how important it is to get to know the young people who are going to be part of your organization and how willing they usually are to share their life experiences with their mentors. This may have been especially true in Obama's case whose father had absented himself from the young man's life, leaving a void to be filled by others.

Because you can't talk about the law all the time, I have learned that another way to evaluate a law student or a junior lawyer is to let them talk about their backgrounds. In this regard, we have no way of knowing what personal information Obama and Tribe shared with one another during their close three-year mentor-mentee relationship at Harvard. But it is reasonable to assume that Tribe heard something about Obama's life narrative from this older, more confident student who had spent years in community organizing work after graduating from Columbia. And regardless of what Tribe and Obama shared with one another, it would be helpful for us to stand back and take a brief look at Obama's life story - as limited as it is - to help determine whether a two term Obama presidency will doom the Rule of Law.

He had a multicultural background and spent some of his formative years in Indonesia. Given the media's unrealistic love affair with Obama's basketball prowess, a look at this chapter in his life may also be informative. Obama played on a state high school basketball championship team in Hawaii. Like many high school athletes who carry some frustration around for the rest of their lives, he may have been a little reluctant to confide that he played second string in part because of his lack of basketball discipline. His "Bobby Knight" like coach did not tolerate Obama's playing style even though Obama lobbied the coach for more playing time.[19] Apparently his basketball coach did not believe the best way to compete for a state basketball championship was to put the star players on the bench to give more playing time to the less talented, undisciplined players in the name of "spreading the wealth around"; a lesson that Obama did not carry forward to help America's economy.[20]

Obama also attended elite liberal schools in the United States - Occidental College in Los Angeles and Columbia University in New York - before arriving at Harvard. And Obama had a Pakistani roommate at Occidental before he transferred to Columbia, who called himself a "socialist." It was this idealistic roommate who believed in economic equality and helped "ignite" Obama politically.[21] Obama visited his friend in Pakistan during his Occidental years and saw how the supposed feudal system operates in Pakistan with the serfs and workers "subservient" to their landlords.[22]

His only experience in a traditional U.S. business setting involved working for about a year, after graduating from Columbia, for a publishing and consulting firm in New York, in 1983–84: Business International Corp. It was a data collection company that produced reports and newsletters for its corporate clients. Obama worked in the "financial services" section, interviewing business experts... [and] following market developments."[23] His innate dislike for the business world, while possibly hidden at the Business International office, was unmistakable. In his memoir he would later admit "[l]ike a spy behind enemy lines, I arrived every day at my computer terminal, checking the Reuters machine that blinked bright email messages from across the globe."[24]

This personal animosity for the world of finance and business - a world that one day he would find himself disparaging while simultaneously regulating as President of the U.S. - is even more evident from a letter that his mother sent to a friend about Obama's post-Columbia work experience:

"Barry is working in New York this year, saving his pennies so he can travel next year. My understanding from a rather mumbled telephone conversation is that he works for a consulting organization that writes reports ... about social, political and economic conditions in Third World countries. He calls it 'working for the enemy' because some of the reports are written for commercial firms that want to invest in those countries."[25]

Obama spent nearly three years as a community organizer in Chicago and had first-hand experience with Chicago Democratic Party politics before he entered Harvard law School. And his rationale for going to the Harvard was not to become an outstanding lawyer but instead "to acquire the tools he needed for politics."[26] To Tribe, it must have been clear that young Barack Obama had tenuous roots into traditional American political and legal principles and a perfect subject for his indoctrination in the ways of liberal legal theory. As we shall see later in this book, mentor Tribe did in fact succeed in shaping Obama's views about the Rule of Law and would even become a confidant and member of his administration.

Obama's Harvard Law School indoctrination, though, would not be limited to his "many hours in Tribe's office" or on their "walks along the Charles river."[27] Courses he would take from self-proclaimed "leftist" and "revolutionary" professor, Roberto Unger, would go even further in laying the foundation for both Obama's understanding of traditional American legal theories and the strategies to undermine rule of law principles.[28] While at HLS, Obama took two courses from Unger, Jurisprudence and a course in his third and final year entitled "Reinventing Democracy." Unger, who has been characterized as more of a "political philosopher" than a "legal scholar" was a leading proponent of a theory that started permeating law schools in the 1970s known as "Critical Legal Studies" or CRITs to some Harvard students, which we will take a hard look at later.[29] Suffice it to say, the proponents of Critical Legal Studies went well beyond teaching the students about the foundation of American law. They believed that the American legal system only "pretends to be consistent and non-ideological and just another level of entrenched power."[30]

In law school, students take jurisprudence early in their three-year curriculum because it concentrates on the basic elements of the American legal system, including the rule of law ideal. To use a sports metaphor, it is where the student learns about the "blocking and tackling" of the law that are necessary for purposes of understanding how the legal system functions. In Unger's jurisprudence course, law student Obama learned - in the words of one of Obama's classmates - Unger's "multi-step argument." They first "inspected and then undermined the presumptions of American legal thought."[31] The characterization that opened this chapter, i.e., that at Harvard Law School, an "ACLU liberal is considered a centrist," couldn't be more apt when one considers that Obama and other Harvard law students were actually receiving intellectual field training in how clever lawyers can undermine the legal system upon which U.S. society is built.

Obama's professor Unger was born in Brazil and later served in the Brazilian socialist government of Luiz Inacio Lula da Silva. Brazil has a tumultuous history of various forms of government, including a military dictatorship and an occasional coup d'état.[32] Teaching about ways to undermine the American legal system from one of Brazil's favorite sons at Harvard Law School speaks volumes about the mind-set of the leadership at the Harvard Law School and the students who would elect to take his courses as Obama did when he signed up for the "Reinventing Democracy" course in his third year. Most of the conventional students, on the other hand, avoided taking the course presumably because of its radical nature.[33] Given such a climate on campus, it is no wonder that Elena Kagan, dean of the law school from 2003 to 2009 - and who would later be appointed to the U.S. Supreme Court by President Barack Obama - took a position against allowing U.S. military recruiters on the Harvard campus.[34]

Unger has acknowledged that he and Obama kept in contact by email and Blackberry up through the 2008 presidential election campaign. His name, radical philosophy and Obama's linkage to both have not become subjects for the evening news inasmuch as Unger has said "I am a leftist, and by conviction as well temperament, a revolutionary…. Any association of mine with Barack Obama in the course of the campaign could do only harm."[35] (Unger was not the only professor who hid part of Obama's history at the Harvard Law School from the public during the 2008 campaign as it might relate to Obama's disdain for the Rule of Law. Charles Ogletree, a Harvard Law School professor who represented Clarence Thomas's accuser, Anita Hill, in the 1991 Supreme Court nomination hearings taught both Obama and his wife Michelle at the law school.[36] In March 2012, a video clip was uncovered on which Ogletree admits to hiding - during the 2008 campaign - a 1990 video of Obama praising and hugging radical professor, Derrick Bell, at a campus rally and asking fellow Harvard students to "open up your hearts and your minds" to Professor Bell.[37] Bell advocated the so-called "Critical Race Theory." Critical race theorists believe that the Rule of Law is a "false promise" and that the American legal system is inherently racist and oppresses minorities. Critical race theorists identify more with the "black power" movement of the 1960s than the non-violent form of integration.[38] They have been characterized as a "lunatic core" by a prominent federal judge.)[39]

In his "Reinventing Democracy" course Professor Unger argued against the "mandarins" who in his view ran "contemporary democratic societies and urged the rethinking of western institutions and urged the adoption of a 'universal social inheritance' that went well beyond the New Deal."[40] Unger taught that the Democratic Party in the U.S. had failed in the second half of the 20th century to "follow-up on the early efforts of the new deal."[41] He went on to combine a "critique of western democracies … and the potential forms democracy could or should take."[42] And he has pointed out that the course was "relatively small and very intense" and that Barack Obama participated "as vigorously on the philosophical as well as the more context oriented part."[43] Unger has admitted that many in his class worried that they would not be able to provide an alternative to the conservative American society of the second half of the 20th century that went beyond Roosevelt's "New Deal" without divine intervention in the form of a "crisis of the dimensions resembling that of the Depression of the nineteen-thirties."[44]

From the perspective of these early 90s students in Unger's class, it appears that they must have cheered when the 2007–2008 financial crisis hit in the U.S. and one of their own from Unger's very "intense" Reinventing Democracy class was at the helm of the American ship of state. His Harvard Law School education had provided him the "tools" to "undermine" this country's legal DNA - the Rule of Law - and thereby *pervert* instead of *"preserve, protect and defend the Constitution"* as he promised when he took the oath of office as President of the U.S. Obama now had an opportunity to start destroying the conservative form of American government that had taken hold in the second half of the 20th century and replacing it with the alternative that, in Unger's mind, would need to go well beyond Roosevelt's New Deal.

The question is how, and if, President Obama would implement such an alternative in a western society - namely the United States - that has a constitution and rule of law ideal that stand in the way of the radical changes that Unger and his students believed would be necessary to cure the democratic ills that America suffers from? In other words, would student Obama develop into a great statesman-lawyer who was a tribute to his Doctor of Laws degree as President of the United States or would he use his Harvard law degree to "doctor the laws" to accomplish a leftist inspired political agenda? That question will be answered as we progress through this book.

But before we go there it may help to linger a moment on a passage from the 2004 edition of Obama's memoir *Dreams from My Father.* Possibly we can glean some insight into whether law student Obama left the campus of Harvard Law School as a young man who would approach the Rule of Law as an objective, dispassionate professional or a "score- settler" who would let his innate biases and preferences overwhelm wisdom and good judgment as a government official?

"I went to Harvard Law School, spending most of three years in poorly lit libraries, poring through cases and statutes. The study of law can be disappointing at times, a matter of applying narrow rules and arcane procedure to an uncooperative reality; a sort of glorified accounting that serves to regulate the affairs of those who have power - and that all too often seeks to explain, to those who do not, the ultimate wisdom and justness of their condition."[45]

These are ominous words in that it appears the author, our current president, has such deep-seeded biases and emotional attachments to class warfare beliefs that he completely ignores, in his characterization, the economic and personal freedoms that our rule of law based society guarantees to all citizens. To mention just a few: the right to be free from the arbitrary coercion of government officials that plagues other societies; the protection of our personal property; the right to buy the products of our choice; the right to a free education; a womb-to-tomb safety net; and the right to practice the religion of our choice. Unfortunately, even 13 years after his graduation from law school it sounds as though that revolutionary Unger's "intense" classroom experience "undermining" the foundations of our legal system may have found a home in Obama's psyche. We shall see.

CHAPTER 2

Aristotle, Cicero And Hayek Testify

The Rule of law is a phrase that rolls out of the mouths of many self-serving politicians and judges more interested in their personal ideology than the law. And it is all too often repeated by unquestioning and gullible media every day. It is usually inserted in a sentence by government officials, without definition or meaning, to give the impression that the speaker is unbiased and objective and that his or her decision is based on fixed and long-standing legal principles as opposed to short-term special interest favoritism. In contemporary times, nothing could be further from the truth.

As lawyers ask jurors to do, we will consider the best evidence to rebut these distortions and misconceptions. We will then be in a position to impeach the credibility or, in other words, cut through the misleading statements of the political class and draw knowledgeable and legitimate inferences from the evidence so that we can reach a verdict. The issue we will decide is whether a second-term Obama presidency will be the death knell for the authentic, historically proven rule of law ideal, which history teaches is one of our most valuable, democratic inheritances, and will Obama in that second term continue to drain your wallet? In other words, will this Harvard-educated lawyer lead our country in an objective, unbiased manner to achieve economic security and growth or will he complete a class warfare, wealth redistributionist agenda and put us all on the "road to serfdom," in the words of F.A. Hayek, the eminent twentieth century political philosopher and economist?

Our brief trip through history shows that the classic understanding of the Rule of Law, and the reasons for it, were brought to us by two of history's great philosophers: Aristotle and Cicero. It is generally accepted that the oft-heard phrase to describe the Rule of Law - a "government of laws, not men" - came from the extraordinary philosopher of classical Greece, Aristotle, nearly 400 years B.C.[1] Aristotle concluded, two millennia before our founders in this country broke away from King George III, that if a society is going to have a measure of personal and economic freedom it would have to establish legal principles to limit the arbitrary will of its rulers. The rule of law ideal, also known as the "supremacy of the law," simply put means that no man or woman is above the law, and it applies equally to everyone whether ruler or ruled.

Aristotle's concerns about the importance of restraining the passions of individuals who govern others, through the rule of law, couldn't be clearer: "And the rule of law ... is preferable to that of any individual. On the same principle, even if it be better for certain individuals to govern, they should be made only guardians and ministers of the law .... Therefore he who bids the law rule may be deemed to bid God and Reason alone rule, but he who bids man rule adds an element of the beast; for desire is a wild beast, and passion perverts the minds of rulers, even when they are the best of men."[2]

And from the renowned lawyer and orator, Cicero, of the classical period of the Roman Republic in first century B.C. - a very prosperous time in Rome's history - "we owe ... many of the most effective formulations of freedom under the law. To him is due the conception ... that we obey law in order to be free, and the conception that the judge ought to be merely the mouth through whom the law speaks." It has been said about Cicero that he showed "freedom is dependent upon certain attributes of the law, its generality and certainty, and the restrictions it places on the discretion of authority."[3]

Contrary to Cicero's wise admonitions, as we will see later, our laws and regulations in the 21st century are anything but "general" and "certain." Some of President Obama's predecessors also occasionally played fast and loose with the Rule of Law. However, with the unprecedented actions he and his political appointee regulators have taken to flaunt the Constitution and stifle economic independence and growth, the Obama administration is making an art form out of rule of law busting laws and regulations resulting in an uncertain and floundering economy. And not surprisingly, their actions often favor special interests - especially environmental and union allies of the Democratic Party. And more judges are routinely avoiding the Rule of Law when they exercise discretion to pick winner and losers in the name of so-called "fairness" and "equality" to "advance contemporary notions of justice."

As the centuries unfolded, it also became clear that the Rule of Law's emphasis on the need to control the passions and biases of "rulers" to protect the "ruled" has roots in Christianity's beliefs in man's fallibility. To profess loyalty to a higher law to keep them in check, kings took oaths during the Middle Ages to place themselves under a higher law. The signing of the Magna Carta in England in 1215 by King John is the most notable example during the Middle Ages of a monarch placing himself under the law whether secular or divine. The oath of office that a President of the U.S. takes when being sworn in is a modern version of this historical precedent.

To our British ancestors we probably owe the greatest debt of gratitude for the rule of law ideal and the personal and economic vibrancy that it encouraged. David Hume, the noted British historian of the 18th century, summed up the Rule of Law's overriding importance. He attributed England's historic progress to its transformation from "a government of will to a government of law."[4] America's founders inherited this ideal. They used it against the mother country when the British, like other rulers over the centuries and politicians today, found it an impediment in dealing with the citizens they ruled. In fact, the Rule of Law became the cornerstone of the Declaration of Independence and our Constitution.

But how do we ensure that the rule of law ideal will be honored by those in power, generation after generation, when we turn over the reins of power to other human beings? In other words, when we turn over the jail keys to the sheriff, how do we guarantee he is not going to arbitrarily lock us up too some day? Successful societies have put in place a combination of "safeguards of individual liberty" to help prevent rulers and judges from abusing power.[5] In the classical period, as Cicero teaches, those safeguards were captured in the attributes of "generality" and "certainty" in laws and restrictions on the use of discretion in decision-making. During the Middle Ages as we have seen, rulers were expected to place themselves and the laws they issued under the higher law of God or nature. But it was the great political scientists among the American colonists who reduced to writing - in the form of the American Constitution - the concept of placing rulers and the laws they enacted under a set of higher, long term written principles to govern the actions of short-term majorities in power.

To recap, it is critical to the viability of the Rule of Law that laws not favor the special interests of the temporary majority in power and that the public voluntarily complies with them over a long period of time to provide stability to society. And the Rule of Law demands more from our rulers than that they simply comply with the Constitution. The Constitution provides some discretion that can be abused by a politician or judge who is more concerned about ideology or personal preferences than the Rule of Law. Along with constitutional protections, it has been found that under the formal view of the Rule of Law, laws should possess certain attributes: they should be enacted following long-established voting procedures and principles and be "general" in nature, instead of focusing on particular individuals or classes; and they should provide "certainty" and "equality of application" to all - the ruler as well as the ruled.[6]

To ensure that laws are enacted that meet basic constitutional and other rule of law attributes, the "separation of powers" principle is imperative. In this connection, specifically as it relates to judges, it demands that they be independent of the other branches of government - the President and Congress. But also we need to guarantee that judges apply the law in real-world cases as it is written - objectively and impartially - to prevent our legal system from morphing from a rule of law foundation to one dominated by the "rule by judges."[7] Alarmingly, as we have already seen in an earlier chapter and will see again later, there is a real danger in the U.S. that ideologues are trying mightily to circumvent these rule of law principles, bypassing the electorate to enter this "rule by judges" world. In this world, there is little doubt that judges following their personal preferences instead of the law will pick winners and losers of their choice in the economic realm. From a personal standpoint, when we sacrifice the Rule of Law for a rule by judges there is little question these unelected saviors of mankind will establish moral or immoral values, depending on your point of view, for the rest of us - from the working man on the factory floor to retirees -under the guise of judicial decisions.

Lest we think that we no longer need to be concerned about modern-day politicians taking advantage of the vulnerability of those over whom they exercise control, recent rule of law writings by Professor

Brian Tamanaha of St John's University School of Law bring us back to reality. As he reminds us, "Preventing government tyranny was a concern in ancient Athens, a concern throughout the Medieval period, and continues to be a concern everywhere today. [And] the need for limitations on government will never be obsolete. The great contribution to human existence of the rule of law … is that it provides one answer to this need."[8]

Thus, the Rule of Law is a time-tested ideal of what the law ought to be to maximize the potential for personal freedom and economic success. Confirming that this conclusion is still valid in the new millennium, the widely respected *Economist* magazine makes it clear that "every rich country, with the exception of Italy and Greece, score well on the rule of law."[9]

Based on my many years practicing law, the importance of providing "certainty," or "predictability" in laws and how they are passed and enforced by government officials cannot be overemphasized. The public needs to interact with one another in business and personal matters with confidence and security. For years, I was counsel to the presidents and other personnel of two of the world's most recognized corporate names - General Motors and Suzuki. There is little question in my mind that the rule of law attributes of "certainty" and the "predictability" that follows, were indispensable factors in their ability to run businesses that employed hundreds of thousands of employees. Conversely, the lack of "certainty" and "predictability" in laws, regulations and judicial decisions - that at critical times affected these companies - and continues to plague the U.S. in 2012, are principal causes of our mass hesitancy to make long- term economic commitments resulting in high unemployment and a sclerotic economy. This is true whether the uncertainty involves decisions from the front office to hire more people in the business world or when a workingman from the factory floor and his family want to purchase or sell a home.

In any complicated litigation, lawyers must rely on expert witnesses to prove their cases. And we will do just that as we weigh the question of this book, i.e., will a two-term Obama presidency be the death knell for the Rule of Law and continue to drain your wallet? In addition to Aristotle and Cicero, we have the works of one of the great legal and economic philosophers of the 20th century, F. A. Hayek, a

British citizen born in Austria, to draw from. In his classics *The Road to Serfdom* and the *Constitution of Liberty*, among others, he showed that by adhering to rule of law principles, lawmakers enhance freedom and economic prosperity by encouraging personal initiative and ingenuity - based on a secure and predictable foundation - for the greatest number of people from all walks of life. This Nobel Prize winning economist, professor at the London School of Economics and the University of Chicago and recipient of the U.S. Medal of Freedom in 1991, was also a source of Margaret Thatcher and Ronald Reagan's successful economic policies.[10]

When we consider the depth of the wisdom expressed in his writings relative to the symbiotic relationship of legal, economic and political issues, there is little doubt why Thatcher and Reagan were followers and their late 20th century economies were so vibrant. Unfortunately for us from the factory floor to the front office Barack Obama has chosen a different route. He has chosen instead to borrow from the doctrines of left-leaning and radical Harvard Law School professors, from the failed - more debt and stimulus - economic theories of 1930s economist John Maynard Keynes - as foisted on the American public by another Harvard academic and chief Obama economic advisor, Larry Summers - and especially from the champion of the unsuccessful government intervention New Deal policies: Franklin D. Roosevelt.

Of Hayek's first notable work, *The Road To Serfdom* published in England in 1944, The New York Times book reviewer said:

"One of the most important books of our generation … It is an arresting call to all well-intentioned planners and socialists, to all those who are sincere democrats and liberals at heart to stop, look and listen."[11]

And of the important themes Hayek addressed in *The Road To Serfdom*, the editor of the book's 2007 republication, Bruce Caldwell, University of North Carolina Professor of Economics, gives us an insight that we should be ever mindful of today in the U.S.:

"Hayek's immediate objective was to persuade his British audience that their heritage of liberal democracy under the rule of law should be viewed as a national treasure rather than an object of scorn, as a vital roadmap for organizing society rather than an embarrassing relic of times gone by."[12]

And of *The Constitution of Liberty* published in 1960, Newsweek magazine's book reviewer proclaimed that the book was "[o]ne of the great political works of our time."[13]

Wearing the hat of an economics scholar, Hayek found that the chances of personal freedom and economic success are maximized when people in society are allowed to "interact" with each other "on their own initiative" in a context where knowledge is "dispersed among a great many people ... who "can also foresee with a high degree of confidence what collaboration they can expect from others." But to ensure the economic success that results from this human synergy, Hayek puts on his doctorate of law mantle and stresses the importance of rule of law principles. In this regard, he finds that laws should "provide protection against unpredictable interference" by government and that such laws "should uniformly apply to all" people in society. In this way, the "lawgiver is not to set up a particular order" - as the regulatory overreach that started with the New Deal of The Roosevelt administration and is accelerating in the current Obama administration demonstrate - "but merely to create conditions in which an orderly arrangement can establish and ever renew itself."[14]

Following Hayek's teaching, the greatest number of people would enjoy the needed flexibility to constantly adjust "to circumstances" with the Rule of Law to guide them and thus be able to plan and coordinate their personal and business activities with "certainty." This leads to the maximum use of the knowledge and resources of millions of citizens in a society and a thriving economy. As Hayek has said: "There is probably no single factor which has contributed more to the prosperity of the West than the relative certainty of the law which has prevailed here."[15]

The benefits of enabling the Rule of Law to unleash the "creative powers of a free civilization," in Hayek's words, from the bottom up can be readily juxtaposed with the impediments present when people have to rely on the limited knowledge and uncertain direction of a few ideologically driven government bureaucrats. These administrative agency bureaucrats - who want to control and plan a welfare state economy from the top down - an economy we are precariously close to in the United States - cannot possibly possess the knowledge and spontaneity necessary to make an economy thrive.

In order for this synergy to be successful, Hayek observed that it could not be achieved by "central direction," which is the ultimate goal of all politicians and regulators who believe that only government programs and control over the economy can ensure economic success.[16] To emphasize his point, Hayek tells us: "It would scarcely be an exaggeration to say that the greatest danger to liberty today comes from ... the efficient expert administrators exclusively concerned with what they regard as the public good .... It is inevitable that this sort of administration of the welfare of the people should become a self-willed and uncontrollable apparatus before which the individual becomes helpless ...."[17]

While Hayek wrote the above passage in 1960, there is little question that his admonition has been playing out in dramatic fashion over the last few decades in the U.S. and is reaching a crescendo in the Obama administration. Today, virtually unaccountable agencies of the federal government make end runs around the Rule of Law to protect special interest favorites and skewed ideologies - such as the Department of Homeland Security (non-enforcement of immigration laws), the Department of Health and Human Services (waivers of Obama Care requirements), Department of Energy (solar panel manufacturers), the Environmental Protection Agency (environmental lobby) and the National Labor Relations Board (unions) to name only a few - while the unsuspecting media and most of the American public stand idly by and watch as their rule of law heritage is chipped away.

But Hayek was a realist and saw the erosion of the Rule of Law happening long before the 21st century. Having traced the history of authoritarian regimes in Germany and Russia and seen first-hand the degradation of rule of law principles in England in the 1940s, as it was tilting toward socialism, he provided us a warning:

"[T]he rule of law will not prevail in a democracy unless it forms part of the moral tradition of the community. A common ideal shared and unquestionably accepted by the majority... But if it is presented as impracticable and even an undesirable ideal and people cease to strive for its realization it will rapidly disappear. Such a society will quickly relapse into a state of arbitrary tyranny."[18]

Hayek unequivocally concluded, as Thatcher and Reagan well understood from his teachings, that the welfare state dominated by class-conscious legislation and the stream of overreaching regulations that follow were antithetical to the Rule of Law. To put it bluntly, the rule of law principles cannot be met when society's wealth is being distributed from one class to another by ideologically driven legislators and welfare state bureaucrats in administrative agencies. And when judges who apply the laws make decisions on factors outside the law as written - as urged by liberal law professors and even Supreme Court justices - any semblance of objectivity and impartiality will be lost. And as history shows after awhile - think immigration, entitlements, taxes, and environmental and labor laws - these laws simply break down like any consumer product, building or nuclear reactor would if they were not properly designed and maintained.

Hayek's works demonstrated a prescience that was largely ignored until Margret Thatcher, also dubbed the Iron Lady, became Great Britain's prime minister and Ronald Reagan became the U.S. president in the 1980s. But today, Obama's actions clearly send a message that the Rule of Law is "impracticable and even ... undesirable" when it gets in the way of his agenda. As we will see in more detail in a later chapter, though, based on the experience of the Iron Lady and President Reagan there is still hope that we can catch ourselves and make a free enterprise economy with a rule of law foundation a reality again in the U.S.

CHAPTER 3

THE PROBLEMS WITH LEGALITY AND HUMAN NATURE

Largely because of the self- serving motivations of government officials and the unquestioning attitude of many in the media we often confuse mere "legality" with laws passed and enforced under the Rule of Law. Authoritarian regimes can enact laws that are "legal" within their governing system regardless of the consequences to a persecuted minority.

While we are a long way from a third world country, there is little question that American politicians do not shy away from using the "legality" rationale to cover a law that cannot meet the rule of law ideal. For example, when a law that reeks of uncertainty and special interest favoritism is rammed through Congress in defiance of long- established voting procedures, with a backdrop of senators being offered millions of dollars for their home states and other special favors for their votes, it can be claimed that the law is "legal." But it unquestionably was not enacted following historically proven rule of law principles. Obama Care is a glaring example of just such a law. It failed the rule of law test, while still being considered "legal" and it took a Supreme Court Chief Justice to rewrite Obama Care, as we will discuss in more detail later, to save the key individual mandate component of the law from being struck down as unconstitutional.

And this distinction between a law that is "legal" and one that meets the Rule of Law could not have been clearer when Obama warned the Supreme Court in early April 2012 against overturning his Obama Care legislation after oral arguments in the Supreme Court did not go well for the government a week before. His comments demonstrated beyond a doubt that, in Obama's view, over 200 years of precedent which holds that it is the Supreme Court and not Congress that decides if a law is constitutional is of little importance if it gets in the way of his agenda. In remarks in the Rose Garden at the White House on April 2, he made the case that Obama Care met his "legality" test regardless of whether it met the Rule of Law and the Supreme Court should get out of the way. Unfortunately for the Rule of Law and for the citizens who depend on its viability, it appears from Justice Roberts's June 28, 2012 Obama Care decision that Obama's attacks got to him.

Early on after oral arguments in the spring of 2012, Obama arrogantly and erroneously chastised the court and warned it against overturning Obama Care while failing to recognize the Supreme Court's historically recognized "judicial review" authority that goes all the way back to the famous *Marbury v. Madison* case of 1803 that law students hear plenty about early in their constitutional law classes. In trying to diminish the importance and authority of the Supreme Court justices, he even referred to the highest court in the land as "an unelected group of people [who] would overturn a duly consti-tuted and passed law." What Obama failed to mention is that in our legal system, which is still a" government of laws and not men," that is exactly what the Supreme Court is supposed to do if Congress (a group of men and women) exceeded its authority under the Constitution (the higher law that protects a citizen's liberty from the passions of Congress and the President).[1] Given Obama's view of the diminished role the Supreme Court should play when it seeks to protect a citizen's basic constitutional rights when they conflict with his "mandate," we should all take heed of what he might have in store for our personal and eco-nomic freedom and the Constitution if he gets the chance to appoint another justice or two to the Supreme Court in his second term. As we shall see in a later chapter, Obama's intimidation of the Supreme Court is a play right out of the Franklin D. Roosevelt playbook. Over 80 years before, another Supreme Court justice, ironically also named Roberts, caved into President Roosevelt's 1930s criticism of the Supreme Court and thereafter started supporting the constitutionality of Roosevelt's New Deal legislation.

Remarkably, though, while we are focusing on the question of "legality" vs. the Rule of Law, we would be remiss if we did not address a current and one of the most glaring examples of a unilateral and unconstitutional power grab by a U.S. President in recent history. As we approach the 2012 presidential election, the Obama administration in its desperate attempt to get reelected appears to have thrown off the necessity of even making a serious attempt at justifying its actions with the imprimatur of so-called "legality." In early January 2012, in an unprecedented move, Obama appointed Richard Cordray, to head the Consumer Financial Protection Bureau - another bureaucracy that was created by the controversial 2010 Dodd-Frank financial system legislation - as well as three members of the National Labor Relations Board. He did so without approval of the Senate or during a Senate recess, as required by the Constitution. The *Wall Street Journal* called Obama's disdain for the rule of law "Contempt for the Constitution" and the so-called "legal rationale for the appointments" from Obama's Justice Department as "junk law."[2]

While Obama makes it sound like he is on the side of the American public when making these appointments, in each case he has ignored the Rule of Law to usurp a little more power not authorized by the separation of powers principles of the Constitution, which clearly delineates the authority possessed by Congress and the President. Ultimately this self-aggrandizing and arbitrary behavior can, and likely will, be used in economically damaging ways such that it can negatively impact all of us. When we can't get a mortgage from a risk-averse bank or we can only use a debit card at a government-favored bank ATM miles from our home, it may turn out that the so-called "fat cat bankers," to use Obama's disparaging words, are not the government's only targets.[3]

The Consumer Financial Protection Bureau – a creature of the Dodd-Frank banking legislation of 2010 - is largely unaccountable and will have the power to stifle financial institutions since it wields control over the institutions and their mortgages, credit cards and other financial products with its vague and draconian authority to declare business practices "unfair, deceptive or abusive." A lawsuit challenging the constitutionality of key parts of the Dodd-Frank law (Wall Street Reform and Consumer Protection Act) was filed in June 2012 by Community banks and other plaintiffs because, as their counsel C. Boyden Grey tells us, the law "violate[s] a bedrock rule of law [principle]: the Constitution's separation of powers, which the Founders designed to limit the growth of government." The plaintiffs argue that the regulators operating under Dodd-Frank will have "virtually unlimited power" and that the law "does not honor the checks and balances" set up in our constitutional system. "It eliminates them." Tellingly, the plaintiffs appear to echo a principal theme of this book when they conclude that "we are taking a stand because we know that the surest protection for consumers and financial stability is the rule of law, beginning with the Constitution."[4]

The CFPB's power to distort the market for financial products - credit and debit cards, etc. and to run roughshod over banks - is likely to result in the same kinds of debilitating product distortions caused by the federal fuel economy standards that were enacted into law in the 1970s. These mandates, which we will get into later, called corporate average fuel economy standards or CAFÉ for decades have forced the sale of revenue draining, heavily discounted small cars to a public that really didn't want them.

The Dodd-Frank legislation is a classic case of government officials passing a bad law (Dodd-Frank) to cover up decades of rule of law mocking legislation and regulations that manipulated the housing market to force and encourage financial institutions to lend to individuals who could not afford to purchase homes. It also covered up the irresponsible actions of former Senator Chris Dodd and Massachusetts Congressman Barney Frank who were the major supporters of the ill-fated Fannie Mae and Freddie Mac, the government sponsored entities at the heart of the crisis.

And most of all, the Dodd-Frank legislation, which Obama claims is one of his most important accomplishments, covers up the colossal breakdown of the Rule of Law. When we look beyond the blame that politicians want to pin on the financial services sector alone we see that the crisis has much deeper implications for our 21st century society. The rule of law breakdown was systemic. It manifested itself, among other things, with rule of law busting legislation and regulations from politicians and bureaucrats who were responsible for an artificial "bubble" in the housing industry due to their policies that encouraged home purchases by those who could not afford them; home purchasers lying about their income, etc. on contractually binding mortgage documents so that they could qualify for mortgages; brokers playing fast and loose with representations to lenders relative to financial health of the purchasers; and, in some cases, financial institutions failing to do their due diligence before they made representations about mortgage securities to potential investors. We didn't need more bad laws to cover up the failures of the past. But instead we needed a full-blown policy initiative led by the President of the United States to once again make the Rule of Law the "moral tradition of the community," the failure of which was one of the root causes of the crisis.

And with respect to the NLRB, as will be discussed in more detail later, it has already been shown during Obama's first term how it can extort union concessions from companies, in this case Boeing. As a result of a lawsuit with little merit filed by the NLRB against Boeing, the NLRB prevented Boeing from building airplanes in a "right to work state" (South Carolina), until it agreed to union demands in pro-union Washington state.

To take a more extreme example, think of authoritarian regimes that convince a gullible public to give them virtually limitless power. Actions taken by those regimes might be "legal" when based on laws passed by a puppet legislative majority but when the laws serve to persecute minorities or the property of one class is expropriated and given to others, they are not acting under the Rule of Law. Owing to our underlying constitutional protections in the U.S., we are somewhat protected from "arbitrary tyranny" but in light of Obama's recent executive overreach in making unauthorized appointments to agencies and bureaus, there is a real question of how much constitutional protection actually exists if a president is going to blatantly ignore its strictures.

Beyond the constitutional questions, when the government picks winners and losers - in a heavily regulated "uncertain "and "unpredictable" economy - driven by a president, legislators and bureaucrats who ignore rule of law principles to achieve welfare state policies - we have driven the economy and our way of life off course. While government officials have always tried to play favorites, in one form or another, it appears to have become more business as usual in the Obama administration than at other times in this country's history, as we will discuss in a later chapter.

And when politicians in contemporary times play fast and loose with the Rule of Law - just like the philosophers of old concluded - we lose more than our personal freedom. Based on empirical or in other words sound statistical evidence, we can conclude that lawmakers who fail to maintain and nurture the Rule of Law are recklessly disregarding the relationship between a country's economic growth and the Rule of Law. In unequivocal terms, MIT researchers have found that in a cross-country study of approximately 100 countries, one of the key "relevant" factors to determine "economic growth" and "stimulants to investment" was the "greater maintenance of the rule of law."[5]

It may help to understand better the seriousness of our legal and economic problems and the damage that is being done daily to much of our economy, to reflect on what could have been in the U.S. over the last few decades if we had not been exposed to these cobbled together, special interest-oriented laws and regulations that have exploded in the last four years. In this regard, we just need to view the tragic state of our affairs from the perspective of one of the few economic success stories in recent U.S. history that is a glaring exception to business as usual in Washington. While much of the U.S business world is suffering from stifling regulations that result, at a minimum, in "uncertainty" and excessive costs, the internet world has so far been spared the heavy hand of the federal government. Think what we would have missed in the technology world if Apple's Steve Jobs would have had to seek approval from administrative agency bureaucrats every time he wanted to develop a new product.

Luckily for Apple and all of us, Congress has not yet enacted legislation that builds in the "uncertainty" and "unpredictability" of multiple layers of regulatory approvals and reporting requirements applicable to Apple products. Obviously, if it had, more of us would still be chained to our land line phones instead of the iPhone and be using computer behemoths instead of the iPad.

If you think the importance of adhering Rule of Law principles instead of just accepting the legality of laws and regulations is something that should be relegated to the history books think again. Stressing the importance of the rule of law attributes of "certainty" and "equality" of application in particular, one of the leading rule of law scholars of the 21st century, Professor Brian Tamanaha, has said: "certainty is one of the most important social benefits conferred by the legal system. And echoing Hayek's findings decades before he tells us that "[i]t allows individuals to plan their activities and coordinate their behavior. In a pragmatic legal system [non-rule of law based] it could not be known whether the legal rules would be applied or set aside. The equality of application principle would also be a casualty."[6]

Clearly legal theorists have criticized the traditional rule of law ideal over the years with the hope of neutering the rule so that it becomes less of a rule and more of a tool to achieve their view of "social objectives."[7]

As any sports fan can appreciate, this would be akin to a referee, turning off the video replay technology, so that he can exercise his own judgment to call a football player in bounds and award a touchdown when the player in reality stepped out of bounds. The other team - the one that does not evoke "social" concerns on the part of the referee - is almost always "out of bounds" in an identical situation. Or one hockey team might get away with an occasional elbow to the head of an opposing player while the out of favor team gets the maximum time in the penalty box for elbowing. The "uncertainty" caused by this kind of ad hoc officiating where the official on the field picks winners and losers through unpredictable and biased rules enforcement would soon lead to boos, a loss of confidence in the sport and drastically reduced ticket sales. The similarities to our current governmental mess based largely on the manner in which our legal system operates couldn't be more evident!

And it has even been said of the anti-rule of law movement led by Obama's Harvard law Professor Unger that "[t]heir goal was to delegitimate the entire system rather than to find ways in which it might work better by ameliorating the flaws they identified."[8] Thus, the critics of the Rule of Law have either not been able to come up with better alternatives or their suggested replacements turn out to be nothing more than doctrines that incorporate utopian-like ends and thus the doctrines cease to be rules at all.

Notwithstanding the lack of alternatives offered by its critics, the rule of law ideal is barely recognizable in contemporary society. Arguably this is in part due to the legal skepticism that permeated the anti-establishment era of the 1960s–1970s which Obama's Professor Unger and others played a large part in fomenting. We can no longer say with confidence that the Rule of Law is part of the "moral tradition of the community" and whether you live in New York City or Kalamazoo, Michigan you probably have little or no idea of the long- term damage to your personal and economic well-being when rule of law principles are undermined. And until, and unless, the persons living on Main Street and Wall Street take a stand at the ballot box, clever politicians and judges have and will continue to dismiss the rule of law ideal with impunity by simply relying on the claimed "legality" of their actions.

While it is encouraging to think of IPhone success stories, unfortunately they are not the reality for much of America's economy, as I have seen up close as the head of the Product Regulation department of the General Motors Corporation Legal Staff in the 1980s and early 1990s. The regulatory assault of the auto industry starting in the late 1960s, along with ever-increasing union demands, that culminated in the bankruptcy of GM in 2009 played a significant role in GM's economic collapse. The reality is that the rule of law ideal in the United States is on life support as special interest focused legislation - unions and environmentalists in GM's case - regulatory overreach and judicial law-making over the last few decades is coming to a "tipping point" in 2012. As a result, the American economy is in a precarious state. Why is that? Why haven't the principles of the great philosophers of classical Greece and Rome, as well as the British scholars of more recent centuries, the drafters of our own founding documents, the renowned thinkers and leaders of the 20th century, such as F.A Hayek, Margaret Thatcher and Ronald Reagan, been followed by many of our political leaders and judges?

It is a given that history shows monarchs and politicians have often - sometimes criminally as Richard Nixon's Watergate demonstrates - tried to skirt the Rule of Law when it became a roadblock to achieving their special interest objectives. In the next chapter, we will see that President Franklin D. Roosevelt showed little respect for the Rule of Law when he tried to pack the Supreme Court with justices favorable to his new deal agenda. While he did not succeed in this reckless Supreme Court "packing" scheme, FDR's intimidation of the Supreme Court, in combination with his excessive regulatory intervention into the lives of all Americans, set the stage for what could be the collapse of the Rule of Law in an Obama second term.

The answer to our question as to why many politicians and judges violate rule of law principles is as old as mankind. And it undermines the beliefs of all who want to place unfettered hope and trust in government officials. The answer can be summed up in two words - human nature - as Aristotle warned us over two millennia ago when he spoke of the "passions that pervert the minds of rulers." And none of us would need biblical precepts and "God's rescue mission at Christmas" in the words of Rick Warren, the pastor of Saddleback Church and the world- acclaimed author of *The Purpose Driven Life*, if man were not fallible. Citing, Isaiah, the great prophet of Israel, Warren reminds his congregation of man's inclination to stray from "God's path to follow our own ways."[9]

Recognizing man's innate fallibility, Hayek's observations about the need for the application of rule of law principles appear right on point, whether we apply them to government officials and judges of the 1930s, those of the 21st century or the decades in between:

"And as we want to prevent the judge from infringing law for a particular reason, so also we want to prevent the legislature from infringing certain general principles for the sake of temporary and immediate aims…. [T]he reason for this need … is that all men in pursuit of immediate aims are apt … to violate rules of conduct which they would like to see generally observed …. In individual as in social conduct we approach a measure of rationality or consistency in making particular decisions only by submitting to general principles, irrespective of momentary needs …. Legislation can no more dispense with guidance by principles than any other human activity …."[10]

CHAPTER 4

FDR SETS THE STAGE FOR OBAMA

While he was beloved by a considerable portion of American society - just as benevolent but often arbitrary kings have been in other times in history -Franklin D. Roosevelt's disdain for the Rule of Law in the 1930s set the stage for an assault on this ideal that we are still feeling today. And once the rule of law's grounding as the "moral tradition of the community," to use Hayek's words, is weakened as it was in the 1930s it is easier for subsequent generations of government officials and judges to avoid or ignore the ideal completely.

The Supreme Court in the 1960s and 1970s brought judicial lawmaking -based on the justices own values as applied to legal principles - to never seen before levels.

We were deluged in the 1970s with so-called consumer-oriented laws and regulations that trampled on rule of law principles of "generality," "certainty," and "equality of application." In our unabashed belief in administrative agencies and the so-called wisdom of bureaucrats, Congress passed laws and presidents signed them that recklessly conferred broad discretionary powers on these unelected bureaucrats.

Many influential law school professors - picking up on the Vietnam-era protest movement and the loss of objective values of the 1960s and 1970s - sought to diminish the rule of law ideal and have thereby created generations of practicing lawyers, government officials and judges who see the law as nothing more than an instrument to be used to fit short-term interests. Our denigration of the Rule of Law and misguided lawmaking over these decades has now come home to roost. By 2012, Roosevelt's 21st century successor, Barack Obama, would be in a position to outdo FDR in undermining the Rule of Law. And after just four years of Obama policies - not to mention the economic carnage that will result from a second term - we are left with an anemic

21st century economy with high unemployment, savaged retirement savings, and more people on food stamps than ever before.[1]

Two fallible *Homo sapiens*, Franklin D. Roosevelt and later Barack Obama, who apparently concluded - even more so than their presidential peers - that they stood above centuries-old principles that underlie the Rule of Law. Like someone who believes he can jump off a cliff and defy the laws of gravity, they both threw aside the importance of the rule of law principles to achieve their own ideologically based agendas. Obviously there are other former presidents who have skirted the Rule of Law - such as Richard Nixon (Watergate) and Bill Clinton (scandals and impeachment process) - but their efforts didn't result in the long-term damage to our rule of law ideal and economy, as Roosevelt's and Obama's initiatives have.

And not surprisingly, along with the suffering that accompanied the failures of the Roosevelt administration in the 1930s, those who have lost their paychecks, particularly among minorities, retirement savings, and ability to sell their homes at a reasonable price in the Obama era have paid a painfully high price for his reckless disregard of sound legal and economic principles. For example, unemployment among African Americans in mid-2011 was over 16%, about twice the national average.[2] And as of December 2011, "1.31 million people ages 75 and older were working, a 25% jump from … 2005," just to make ends meet.[3]

History demonstrates that the Rule of Law goes hand in hand with personal freedom and a successful free enterprise economy. With the "certainty" ensured by the Rule of Law - to name just one of its attributes - property and contractual rights are protected. And business and individuals have the opportunity to thrive when people can make long and short- term business and personal plans with confidence that "unpredictable" government interference will not thwart their objectives. When a politician has an agenda to undermine the Rule of Law he or she is, at bottom, undermining a vibrant free enterprise way of life and hurting everyone in society.

But "unpredictable government interference" did not bother the Roosevelt administration, as we will see in more detail below, and it surely does not bother the Obama administration, when his favored special interests' agendas are at stake. For example, in a shocking exercise of meritless and overreaching discretion, in early January 2012,

Obama "stunned investors" by denying a permit for TransCanada's Keystone XL Pipeline that would cut through the U.S. resulting in "20,000 direct and 100,000 indirect jobs along the pipeline." His decision, premised on alleged environmental grounds, comes after the State Department had issued three environmental impact statements over a three year period finding that the project presented "no significant impact" on the environment. There is little question that Obama's decision to delay this project at least another three years was made to appease the environmental lobby even though the company building the pipeline had spent "1.9 billion dollars over 40 months carefully adhering to the federal regulatory process."[4]

The Wall Street Journal did not mince words when it likened Obama's action to that of "Banana republics [which] have trouble attracting capital because of a reputation for arbitrarily changing the rules whenever it suits the populist in power." So if you are one of the 120,000 - many of whom I'm sure are pipefitters - who were counting on a pipeline job, forget it. Paying back the environmental lobby and courting their 2012 votes is more important than your rule of law rights and food on your table. And the Journal also cautions that what is "unseen" by the general public, but not to be missed by investors is the most dangerous aspect of his denial. "Seeing how our president has behaved" the Journal warns, "they [investors] are not likely to come away feeling confident about the rule of law."[5]

The Great Depression of the 1930s presented Franklin D. Roosevelt a crisis of singular proportions in this nation's history from which to create his own government interventionist agenda. To accomplish his agenda, Roosevelt would make an end run around the historically proven rule of law attributes, not to mention concerns about the U.S. Constitution, to re-make America in his image. And, as we shall see, Obama learned well from FDR just what he needed to do to help him march toward making America more of a "government of men," rather than a "government of laws."

Justifying sweeping federal powers in the name of the crisis, Roosevelt initiated the welfare state in the U.S. Roosevelt's New Deal legislation authorized an avalanche of new administrative agencies - with ideologically motivated political appointees at the controls - that wielded broad discretionary powers to implement the legislation and control the lives of virtually everyone in America. And let there be no mistake, the effects of crisis- generated "political discretion" have long lasting damaging consequences on the Rule of Law and our society.

Recalling the statement of Rahm Emmanuel, who would become President Obama's Chief of Staff, that politicians should "[n]ever allow a crisis to go to waste," a leading contemporary authority on the linkage between the rule of law and the economy warns that "[i]n times of economic crisis, unleashing political discretion … is highly destructive of the rule of law…. The crisis becomes the excuse for any and all political agendas that can plausibly (or even implausibly) be linked to the crisis. More importantly, discretion to address the crisis provides cover for identifying political winners and losers and favoring political supporters while punishing others …." He goes on to highlight how destructive Roosevelt's crisis- inspired New Deal legislation and regulatory intrusion into American society in the 1930s and '40s was to the Rule of Law and the economy. In Roosevelt's New Deal, "[t]he federal government seized broad discretionary control, which was supposed to improve the economy. In reality, the endless ill-conceived experimentation made the economy worse, not better. After the Great Depression, the constitutional constraints on government that were temporarily suspended were never re-imposed."[6]

And it is not hard to see the parallels between the denigration of the Rule of Law and the economic stagnation of the Great Depression and the current Great Recession. The unfettered discretion exercised by the Great Depression politicians bred a level of "uncertainty" that paralyzed much of the economy just as it has under the Obama administration. As prolific author and renowned economist, Robert Higgs, concludes in his work on the Great Depression, it was not until the end of World War II in 1945 when the "uncertainty among investors about the security of their property rights," that was caused by Roosevelt's earlier New Deal policies, gave way to the increased investment that brought America out of the doldrums of the Depression.[7]

The long-term significance of Roosevelt's transformation of the U.S. - from a free enterprise economy based on the Rule of Law to a government of bureaucrats in Washington - was also not lost on President Reagan. In this regard, Ronald Reagan placed responsibility for our current regulatory overreach and government-dominated economy at FDR's doorstep. As he said in his 1990 memoir "With his alphabet soup of federal agencies, FDR in many ways set in motion the forces ... to create big government and bring a form of veiled socialism to America."[8]

And Roosevelt's use of the "executive order" to bypass Congress in order to run the government his way is unmatched. In his first two terms Roosevelt signed over 2000 executive orders.[9] He was also the first American president to skirt the Rule of Law by appointing individuals - called "czars" - to important government positions without seeking senate approval, as required by the Constitution. He appointed 11 czars in 12 years. To show how well Barack Obama has learned from Roosevelt's lead, Obama has appointed 38 "czars" in just three years. And if one is interested in the more rule of law oriented performance of Ronald Reagan, he appointed just one czar in eight years![10]

Tragically for the American public during the Great Depression era - whether one worked on the factory floor or front office - his suffocating legislative, regulatory and judicial New Deal agenda, during his first eight years in office, as we have seen above, resulted in the perpetuation of the depression. As an omen of what is to come in an Obama second term, at the end of the 1930s after eight years of the New Deal agenda, the unemployment rate was still pitifully high with millions out of work. Historian Robert McElvaine recounts this dismal time: "In 1939, a full decade after the Crash, 9.4 million Americans remained unemployed. The figure constituted 17.2 percent of the work force. Few would have predicted it in the heady days of 1933, or even in 1935 or 1936 (and many people fail to realize it today), but the Great Depression outlived the New Deal."[11]

But for the national crisis America faced in the early 1940s at the start of World War II and the necessity it brought to overcome the Nazi war machine, there is no telling how much longer the failed New Deal policies would have lasted. While history views Roosevelt as our indispensable war time leader, it was William Knudsen, the president of General Motors, who was tapped by Roosevelt in 1940 to lead the industrial production effort for our World War II defense program. And that successful effort was not accomplished by more New Deal-like programs that stressed "comprehensive, centrally directed plan[s]" and a "war production czar" as many in Roosevelt's administration believed were necessary. Instead Knudsen insisted that Roosevelt "clear away antiquated anti-business tax laws and regulations" and "reduce Washington interference in the production process to a minimum."

Knudsen's "decentralized" approach that relied on the private sector to build the weapons necessary to defend this country was so successful that by "the end of 1942 we were producing more tanks, ships, planes and guns than the entire Axis" (Germany and its allies). And once freed of the New Deal constraints and "unleashed to help win the war, American business enterprise had been brought back to life, and in 1945 it was ready to convert from making machine guns to washing machines and tractors again .... Private investment came roaring back, triggering steady economic growth that pushed the U.S. into a new era, as the most prosperous society in history." Unfortunately for all Americans, Obama's so-called vaunted education failed to teach him the lessons that this country learned in the 1940s that were instrumental in bringing us out of the Great Depression.[12]

Roosevelt's overreaching New Deal approach to the Rule of Law, though, was not limited to legislation, regulations, executive orders and czars. When some of his New Deal legislation was blocked by the U.S. Supreme Court he concocted "judicial reform" legislation. After he won re-election in 1936, Roosevelt decided to "pack" the Supreme Court with additional justices favorable to his New Deal legislation above and beyond the nine sitting justices. It was his hope that he could capture all three branches of the government since the Democrats already controlled Congress and the Oval Office and effectively end opposition to his agenda by gutting the heart of the separation of powers principle enshrined in the Constitution. While Obama has had to live with a divided Congress from 2010-2012, many would argue that he, like Roosevelt, also wants to fill the Supreme Court with ideologically like-minded justices to weaken the separation of powers structure of American government.

Roosevelt's court-packing scheme was eventually voted down by a Senate majority from his own party. The adverse Senate Judiciary Committee Report of 1937 is telling. It is one of the most direct tributes to the Rule of Law and its overriding mission to ensure a "government of laws" over a government dominated by the "will of men" that we have seen from government officials themselves in recent U.S. history. And it levels a clear and unmistakable rebuke of Roosevelt and his attempt to weaken the Rule of Law through manipulation of the Supreme Court. It calls FDR's court- packing plan "a needless, futile and utterly dangerous abandonment of constitutional principle ...

without precedent or justification."[13] And the report emphasizes that the American constitutional system is 'immeasurably more important ... than the immediate adoption of any legislation however beneficial." It goes on to highlight the importance of maintaining "the continuation and perpetuation of government and rule by law, as distinguished from government and rule by men," and grounds its conclusions by proclaiming that we are "re-asserting the principles basic to the Constitution of the United States."[14]

The Senate committee also echoed fundamental and timeless concerns first expressed by Aristotle about the fallibility of government leaders and the overarching need for "certainty" in our legal system:

"The courts are not perfect, nor are the judges. The Congress is not perfect, nor are the senators and representatives. The Executive is not perfect …. We shall destroy the system when we reduce it to the imperfect standards of the men who operate it. We shall strengthen it and ourselves, we shall make justice and liberty for all men more certain when, by patience and self-restraint, we maintain it on the high plane on which it was conceived….Inconvenience and even delay in the enactment of legislation is not a heavy price to pay for our system. Constitutional democracy moves forward with certainty rather than speed."[15]

The Senate Judiciary Committee report itself, though, does not do justice to the level of congressional concerns about Roosevelt's court-packing threat to our democratic way and the rule of law. These concerns are succinctly captured below in McElvaine's history of the Great Depression. While some would think it impossible, others might believe it is not much of a reach to conclude that similar concerns might lie ahead for our 21st century America if Obama is re-elected:

"A second term presidency normally begins to lose leverage with Congress since members of his party do not expect him to be again heading a ticket on which they will run. This process was rapidly accelerated in Roosevelt's case because of his ill-advised introduction of court reform. To many on Capitol Hill, already upset at the flow of power down Pennsylvania Avenue, Roosevelt's attempt to pack the Court raised the possibility of dictatorship in democratic garb."[16]

While we can send a thank you to the congress of 1937, which was dominated by Roosevelt's own Democratic party allies for standing up for the rule of law, there is a real question as to whether the Harry

Reid-led Democratic Party majority in our current Senate would have the character and courage to rebuke Obama in the same way. And in fact, given the way Obama, Reid and Pelosi manipulated congressional voting procedures in 2010 to pass Obama Care, I guess we know for sure what the answer to our question would be.

Notwithstanding the Senate Report's resounding words of praise for the Rule of Law and criticism of those who weaken it, Roosevelt still succeeded in intimidating at least one member of the conservative majority of the Supreme Court, ironically named Roberts, into buckling and voting to uphold his New Deal agenda. That was all he needed. This famous about face on the court was euphemistically referred to in the press at the time as the "switch in time that saved nine" and it can be argued that his intimidation efforts resound to this day.[17]

And if we think that this history does not affect the regular guy on the street and is only for law books - think again. Within a few short years of Roosevelt's court "packing" intimidation efforts, the Supreme Court decided a case that has ever since set the outer bounds for the federal government's power to regulate commerce in the U. S., such as whether the government can order Americans to purchase health insurance under Obama Care. By 1942, the Supreme Court was much more in tune with Roosevelt's agenda and went so far in the opposite direction to uphold a government penalty on a small Ohio wheat farmer for growing 12 acres of wheat above his Department of Agriculture Depression-era wheat acreage allotment.

In *Wickard v. Filburn*, a case that law students learn about early in their constitutional law courses, the court ruled that the federal government's constitutional authority "to regulate commerce … among the several states", in other words "interstate commerce," extended so broadly that it could penalize a farmer who grew a few acres of extra wheat on his farm. It also meant little to the court that the wheat was for purely local use to feed his own poultry and livestock and that his farming didn't have any direct effect on "interstate commerce."[18] The *Wickard* case was relied upon by the government in its efforts to convince the Court to uphold Obama Care under an expansive reading of the "commerce clause."

The Obama Administration, in the end, was successful in convincing a majority of the justices on the Supreme Court to uphold the constitutionality of Obama Care but for a much different reason.

In the June 2012 Supreme Court decision, the states that challenged Obama Care did not have to worry about the overly broad *Wickard* precedent that may, in part, owe its genesis to Presidential intimidation and Supreme Court justices who wanted to be on the Roosevelt side of the political equation. Chief Justice Roberts sided with the liberal faction of the Court and, in effect, rewrote Obama Care to call the unconstitutional "penalty" for violating the individual mandate a constitutionally permissible "tax."[19] He agreed with the opponents of Obama Care that the government did not have power under the "commerce clause" to force someone to buy health insurance or pay a "penalty." But in an exercise of judicial interpretation that has been referred to as a "sleight-of-hand," Chief Justice Roberts miraculously side-stepped years of precedent and other constitutional limitations on the government's power to "tax" and concluded that the government did have authority to tax those who fail to purchase health insurance.[20] Thus, succumbing to Obama's Supreme Court intimidation efforts, as the Roosevelt-era court had decades before when FDR applied the pressure, he saved Obama's individual mandate from the cutting floor and stepped on the Rule of Law in doing so.

And as we reflect upon FDR's damaging rule of law legacy and where Barack Obama may take us, we should keep in mind what happens when the Rule of Law ceases to be part of the "moral tradition of the community." From top to bottom an entire society is corrupted and weakened. Its citizens then become ready subjects for the clever politician with a government takeover agenda. When the rule of law is in a weakened state the men or women in power turn to arbitrary "planning" to achieve their predetermined "ends." A public - without known rule of law standards to apply to their rulers - do not even realize there is a better, proven alternative to government dominance and incompetence. We are then in a state of affairs where we have traveled a long way toward a "government of men "and not a government of laws."

CHAPTER 5

VIETNAM PROTESTS AND THE CRITS

It was a brief 16 years between President Roosevelt's death in 1945 and the end of World War II before the Rule of Law started receiving its next frontal assault in the early 1960s. And the aftershocks are being felt to this day.

The Vietnam era protest and anti-establishment movement in general swept across university campuses in the 1960s and 1970s like a tidal wave. I was in undergraduate school and law school in the 1960s so I have no difficulty understanding the significance of the shock waves that still reverberate from this period. While the level of turmoil and campus disruption varied among universities, all one had to do was visit another university or speak with one of your friends at another school to appreciate what they were experiencing. And the public in general was not spared the television scenes that were exciting the passions of the protesting college students. The nightly news was replete with pictures of shot-down helicopters, soldier death tolls, prisoners of war and propaganda not only from North Vietnam but also from a few left-leaning Hollywood stars as well.

To add to the already fragile state of American society, President John Kennedy was assassinated in 1963; his brother Robert was murdered on the primary campaign trail in 1968 and civil rights leader Martin Luther King was also murdered in 1968. Domestic violence played out in the streets of our cities too as buildings were bombed by groups like the Weather Underground, a self- described communist revolutionary group, once headed by Obama supporter Bill Ayres.[1]

"Law was caught up in the thick of this national schism."[2] Those who were left-leaning politically believed that the law favored the establishment as opposed to the protesters. And they claimed that the police and National Guard were always too quick to break up sit-ins and marches. On the other side of the political spectrum, more conservative voices believed that "rampant civil disobedience encouraged disrespect for the law and threatened social disorder … reaping further lawlessness."[3]

Some so-called elite law schools were not immune to the turbulence that surrounded them. Legal theories that denigrated the importance of the stability and "certainty" afforded by rule of law principles sprang up at these law schools during this tumultuous time. The Critical Legal Studies movement (CRITS) that viewed the law as nothing more than "politics" was born out of this social conflagration.[4] They saw the law as "merely another level of entrenched power, a way of enforcing the primacy and perquisites of the wealthy, the powerful, and the white."[5]

The founding members of the movement were law students at elite institutions during the 1960s and new law professors during the 1970s …. The philosophical prophet of the movement, Roberto Unger, published … *Law in Modern Society* (1976), an elaborate account of the decline of the rule of law …, launching the initial fusillade against … the rule of law."[6] In characterizing the extent of the movement's effort to denigrate the rule of law, another scholar goes so far as to proclaim that "Critical Legal Studies launched an especially radical attack…and that Unger "endors[ed] the dismantlement of the rule of law."[7]

Recall that Unger, the self- proclaimed revolutionary professor, would teach Obama a little over a decade later the ins and outs of "undermining" the rule of law in his Jurisprudence course as well as the "Reinventing Democracy" course that "conventional" students at Harvard Law School avoided. He even went so far as to urge the adoption of a "universal social inheritance" that went well beyond the New Deal. He would also continue to be one of Obama's closet confidants by "email and Blackberry" at least through the 2008 campaign.[8]

And Obama did not leave his CRITS movement indoctrination to Unger alone. As one of his Harvard classmates has said: "Barack didn't study directly with Horowitz and Kennedy [two other Harvard CRIT professors] but they were very much in the air and he absorbed what was going on …." But he conceded that, "[t]he CRIT who was most important to his studies … was Roberto Unger."[9] We should take note that the stuff that was "in the air" - to use Obama's classmate's words of what Obama was absorbing - would make a freedom loving American's hair stand on end. Based on Harvard professor and fellow CRIT leader

Kennedy's writings, it seems he was giddy about the prospect of the decline of the rule of law. He boldly proclaimed, "[t]he decay of the rule of law points the way to an egalitarian Utopia, and rather than lament its decline we should rejoice in the new political opportunities suggested by it."[10]

Obama learned well from his Harvard CRITS professors. The rule of law principles of "generality" (not favoring one class over another) and "equality of application" obviously mean about as much to our president as it did to his professors. For example, Obama had the audacity to lecture the American public, as he did in his January 24, 2012 State of the Union address, about giving everyone a "fair shot." It appeared not to bother Obama at all that this so-called "fair shot" would come to many, now about 50% of eligible taxpayers - who pay no federal income taxes at all - by redistributing the wealth of those families and small businesses making over $1 million per year. This expropriation of one class's income to give to another would be accomplished by trying to cripple those families and small businesses that earn over $ 1 million a year with confiscatory and growth stunting 30% taxes, with few deductions. Since the media do not seem capable of identifying the perfidy in this proposal, he and his allies must be "rejoicing in the political opportunities" that have resulted from the "decay of the rule of law."[11]

What the CRITS of the world failed to emphasize is that the Rule of Law is the foundation of the individual dynamism that drives our free enterprise economy and helps put everyone to work whether on the factory floor or in the front office. At bottom, for the individual or business to make long- term financial commitments that stimulate an economy, they must be able to rely upon laws that apply equally to all in an unshakeable, certain and predictable manner. Unger's CRITS ideology, though, is laced with images of businessmen or other officials as "mandarins" or in other words the "elite." And he seems preoccupied by the so-called prevalence of "unjustifiable power" in our society.[12]

We should also not think that Obama was just a passive observer in class. As Unger concedes, Obama participated "as vigorously on the philosophical as well as the context oriented part."[13] With this indoctrination, in combination with Obama's innate disdain for business and the law in general as evidenced by his *Dreams From my Father* memoir, it is no wonder that he tries to blame the "greed of a few" for the U.S. financial crisis and stokes the fires of class warfare in his speeches.[14]

The revolutionary beliefs that Unger instilled in Obama and his other students were unequivocal and contrary to our rule of law tradition. In this connection, Unger proclaimed in *Law in Modern Society* that the "vicissitudes of class struggle strip the state of every pretense to impartiality." And that Karl Marx - the intellectual pioneer of the communist movement - is one of "the most profound, social thinkers of the modern age." If these are your beliefs and you are spending hours each day indoctrinating students in such beliefs, then philosophically you do not want to see the rule of law and the free enterprise economy it supports succeed.[15] Consequently, the more that the attributes of the rule of law -generality, certainty and equality - can be undermined, the more difficult it becomes for a free enterprise economy to thrive.

So with the turmoil of the 1960s and early 1970s as the crisis to use as the excuse to change the rule of law based system in the U.S., - about a decade before Obama would sign up for Professor Unger's classes - Unger made a name for himself as a radical professor when he published *Law in Modern Society*, a book that seemed to revel in the decline or hoped for decline of the Rule of law. He also laid out a frightening alternative to a society based on the Rule of Law; one that sacrifices individual freedom on the altar of community "solidarity."[16] A review of Unger's book gives us a good perspective into his roadmap for undermining the Rule of Law and the radical "community" alternative he proposes as its replacement. It's also obvious from his radical teachings and Obama's full participation in his classes why he and Unger kept his ongoing relationship with Obama out of the media spotlight during the 2008 campaign.[17]

What is telling about Unger's methodology, which is consistent with Obama's classmate's characterization of Unger's teaching, is that Unger clearly sets out key legal principles upon which the rule of law depends. Then he unmistakably highlights a rationale for how such principles have been or can be undermined. All of this for the purpose of leading up to a proposed community "solidarity" alternative that would replace the rule of law based society upon which our government and economy was founded. This "chilling" alternative would supplant the "demise the rule of law" by re-asserting concerns of the community. His form of utopia is supposedly necessary to overcome the "unjustified power" that exists in a society in which individual initiative and competition thrive.[18]

We might ask at this point whether the CRITS' philosophy could be the underlying platform for the "change" that candidate Obama so boldly, yet vaguely proclaimed during the 2008 campaign and that we are hearing about again in 2012? But now that his economic plans of the first term have failed, Obama is desperately putting a little more meat on the CRITS' revolutionary bones when he sprinkles misleading statements about the rich and elites - designed to inflame passions - in his campaign rhetoric. For example, when Obama said in his January 24, 2012 State of the Union address and repeated on the campaign trail the next day that millionaires and billionaires should "pay as much in taxes as a secretary," he is demeaning the office of the president by resorting to the semantic tricks of slick trial lawyers who try to prejudice a jury with misleading statements that do not have hard evidence to support them. Among successful businessmen as a group, that the CRITS were so hostile to, he was obviously taking a shot at one of their elites -Republican presidential candidate Mitt Romney - when he made his taxes claim during his January 24, 2012 State of the Union address. For theatrical purposes, Warren Buffett's secretary even sat in the gallery.

But Romney's 2010-2011 tax returns show that he paid $6.2 million in taxes for those tax years. And that he gave approximately $7 million to charity on income of about $43 million.[19] Thus, if the media were on their toes and had a modicum of courage they would challenge Obama's veracity every time he says that millionaires don't "pay as much in taxes as a secretary" by simply using Romney's tax payments to the IRS as an example. Someone might also want to give Mr. Romney a pat on the back for his extraordinary contributions to charity, especially to his church which received about $4 million from Romney and his wife. They obviously have put in practice the Bible's instruction that we should tithe and give 10% back to the Lord.

While we don't have hard data on Warren Buffett's secretary's taxes, based on her income range a gross assessment of her possible tax payments can be made. In this connection, it has been assumed, based on her alleged tax rate, that she is paid a salary of between $200,000 and $500,000 per year.[20] It has also been reported that her tax rate is approximately 34%.[21] And, for the sake of argument, let's just assume that she pays anywhere between $68,000.00 and $170,000 in annual tax payments to the IRS. Mr. Obama, that's a long way from Mitt Romney's tax payments of roughly $3 million per year.

If you also consider the misleading tax rate argument that Obama and others like to make, Mitt Romney still makes Buffett's secretary's rate look more appealing. Mitt Romney's income - that was largely based on investments was taxed twice - once when the corporation he invested in paid its taxes - possibly as much as 35% -on the money investors like Romney put to work in the company and again at 15% when Romney paid capital gains or dividend taxes on the same money. In effect, Romney's income - after it has passed through the corporation and back out to the shareholders who put their money into the corporation in the first place - is taxed at a rate approaching 50%.[22] So even on the rate argument, Obama's claims have the odor of a "hustle" from a lawyer who should know better based on the law and facts. These are the kinds of half- truth arguments that we see so often in litigation when trial lawyers try to run such ginned up representations past judges and juries, unless and until opposing counsel objects or the court eventually sanctions them for their repeated violations of the court's rulings. While we can't sanction a president short of impeachment, voters can take the measure of the president's truthfulness at the ballot box.

And what this little detour into Mitt Romney's and Buffett's secretary's taxes might also teach us is that we should praise our marvelous economic system because enough business revenue was generated such that Warren Buffett could afford to pay his secretary between $200,000 and $500,000.00 per year. Instead of demeaning the rich as Obama does when he makes his class warfare speeches, he should be looking for more ways to create future Warren Buffetts who can accumulate enough wealth so that they can afford to pay hundreds of thousands of dollars to a secretary. In short, he should be more like Margaret Thatcher, as we will see in a later chapter, and be more concerned about making the "poor richer" rather than trying to make "the rich less rich."

So what else can we learn from the self-proclaimed revolutionary's book *Law in Modern Society* that might shed some additional light on why Barack Obama thinks so little of the Rule of Law? There is little question that Unger understands the importance of the Rule of Law in a democratic society. Starting with the manner in which laws are made by legislators -whether they serve at the state level or in Congress - Unger explains that one interpretation of the Rule of Law "makes certain demands on the method of legislation itself. It requires that laws be made by a procedure to which everyone might have reason to agree in his own self interest." But in the next breath, he lets the reader and the crafty politician appreciate how much can be gained by undermining this pre-eminent principle: "procedure is inseparable from outcome: every method makes certain legislative choices more likely than others, even though it may often be difficult to spot its bias on any given matter."[23]

Let's just shine a spotlight on the way Obama and the Reid Pelosi-led Congress rammed the final Obama Care bill through congress in 2010 - after Senator Ted Kennedy passed away and the Democrats lost their filibuster- proof majority. They used arcane budget procedures that only required 51 votes to pass the final amended Obama Care bill through the Senate instead of the 60 votes needed to avoid the long-established senate filibuster related voting procedures. Upon reflection, we can clearly spot the "bias" to use Unger's word in their maneuvers. There is little question that the Obama-Reid-Pelosi voting procedures manipulation fit neatly into Unger's teachings about ways to under-mine the Rule of Law. It surely determined the outcome of Obama Care because the Democrats did not have the sixty votes needed for passage in the senate in early 2010.

Unger also makes clear that regulatory law, as enforced by unelected bureaucrats, undermines the Rule of Law. He proclaims it can and will be violated whenever the governing authorities [think the Department of Energy and the Solyndra solar panel maker scandal in our current administration] believe the Rule of Law gets in the way of "the political interests of the rulers."[24] And that, as a society places more emphasis on becoming a "welfare state," it further diminishes the effectiveness of the Rule of Law. In a welfare state, says Professor Unger, governing officials have to assume "managerial responsibilities" over the governed to remedy so-called past wrongs caused by private enterprise. When this happens the administrators cannot possibly manage the affairs of their agencies to achieve "substantive justice" - as the left calls redis-tribution of wealth - and still apply general rules to everyone as the rule of law ideal calls for.[25] So the Rule of Law is a casualty again. In Unger's words, the "governmental distribution" that results from the welfare state administered by regulators "are never impartial and general enough to have anything more than the appearance of law."[26]

Unger does not forget about the judges' role in his treatise on the Rule of Law and how they have or can undermine rule of law principles. As the judge seeks to reach "substantial justice," Unger says he will have to interpret a rule "to choose the most efficient means to the attainment of the ends one assigns to it."[27] This approach to judging is called "purposive legal reasoning." It results in a wide variety of different decisions based on the ends or "purposes" the judge believes are best served in a case. The overarching purpose for the judge in a welfare state society, as we are becoming in the U.S., is to achieve "social justice" whether he meets the Rule of Law or not. Basically, what Obama's professor seems to be saying is that as the regulators stray from the Rule of Law in the welfare state to accomplish their ideological agenda, then the courts will be more inclined to accommodate the regulators by distorting the judicial decision's rationale to fit the regulators so-called "social justice" purpose. This is a classic case of the "ends justifying the means" with the Rule of Law being the casualty.

Obama's regulators are marching right in step to Unger's teaching. For example, the Department of Housing and Urban Development (HUD), in late January 2012, hurried to issue a rule "forcing banks to lend to minorities." HUD is "pushing through a rule to support racial loan quotas a few months before the Supreme Court will rule on whether that's legal." This is all happening in the wake of one of the worst financial crises since the Great Depression that was largely caused by the same fanatical interest on the part of the government to force banks to make mortgage dollars available to people who could not afford homes. But Obama's HUD does not seem to even appreciate the economic damage that such rule of law denigrating action will cause in its "unseemly rush to issue a rule in a bid to sway the their [Supreme Court] decision."[28]

This so-called "purposive" legal reasoning that Obama and his acolytes at HUD hope the Supreme Court will adopt as the "means" to accomplish their "ends," is the opposite of the impartial objective decision-making sought by the Rule of law - that is applying general rules to the facts regardless of the outcome. Under this so-called "purposive" legal reasoning approach, one that is espoused by Supreme Court justice Stephen Breyer and by Obama, Unger clearly admits that it fails to meet rule of law criteria: "Hence, the very notion of stable areas of individual entitlement and obligation, a notion inseparable from the rule of law ideal, will be eroded.[29]

Thus, there is little question that Unger provided his students the background and understanding of the rule of law ideal that would allow them to "hack into" the code of the ideal and eat away at its principles with the CRITS' virus. And from the earliest days of the Obama administration, the rule of law has been under vigorous attack. (As a portent of things to come in a second term, though, it appears that his radical guru, Professor Unger, does not believe Obama has gone far enough in his leftist soak- the- rich campaign. In a recent YouTube video, Unger severely criticized Obama, his former student, ostensibly for not taking America far enough to the left to punish the "moneyed interests" in his first term. He even ranted that because of his failures to the progressive movement, Obama should be defeated in 2012. So if you think Obama's first term resulted in an affront to the Rule of Law and our free enterprise economy, as we have shown in the pages of this book, hold on to your seats because his leftist intellectual heroes are sending him clear messages about how much more radical his post-2012 agenda should be, if he wins reelection.)[30]

The Vietnam protest era's effects on the law, though, were not limited to just a few universities and to the CRITS philosophy alone. According to Professor Tamanaha, "[A] dramatic transformation" took place in the 1960s and 1970s. "Law school enrollment doubled in that period, boosted by an influx of many entrants not particularly interested in practicing law. The next generation of law professors …" from the elite law schools was drawn from this group of students. They "identified themselves as scholars, as social and legal theorists, as philosophers … as anything but lawyers."[31] When one considers the overwhelming impact that some of the so-called elite law schools have on legal education and the views of future lawyers toward the Rule of Law, one sees clearly how the minds of generations of lawyers can be shaped in a few decades. In 2005 alone, "Harvard and Yale graduates together supplied one third of all newly hired law professors across the nation; add graduates from Columbia, New York University and Chicago, and the total is one half of all law professors hired."[32]

They took with them a view of the law that was oriented toward the "ends justifying the means" instead of rigorously following fixed principles in legal decision-making to discover the law and then apply it to the facts of a case without regard to the ends. This "instrumental" approach to the law would so permeate our legal system that a leading rule of law authority indicates that we now have "a legal system that is pervasively characterized by lawyers who ignore the binding quality of rules to instrumentally manipulate legal rules and processes without restraint on behalf of their clients ends or their own interests."[33]

Beyond the "transformation" taking place in the law schools in the 1960s and 1970s, society in general was adrift. As author and philosopher Richard Tarnas put it "In the course of the twentieth century society at large underwent a general loss of belief in objectively existing principles."[34] Unfortunately for all of us, when society is adrift and many in the legal profession believe that the law is simply an instrument to be manipulated for one's personal or ideological agenda, it makes it much easier for those who would seek to neuter the Rule of Law to succeed.

CHAPTER 6

NOTRE DAME RULE OF LAW CERTAINTY FOR DISRUPTIVE 1960s PROTESTERS

While the Vietnam crisis was a backdrop to the radical theories of the Harvard Law School CRITS, is there anything positive we can take away from this era? If we could turn back the clock to the 1960s, is there something those years can tell us relative to the way other leading universities dealt with the campus turmoil of the 1960s that might still be relevant to our long-term concerns about the viability of the Rule of Law in a second-term Obama presidency? Were there viable alternatives to the disruption and turmoil on college campuses that so impacted a generation of law students and eventual professors that it shapes and distorts our law to this day?

I was spared the disruption on university campuses in the late 1960s that led to the legal skepticism of the 1970s at the so-called elite schools, including Columbia and Harvard, to name two. I graduated from the University of Notre Dame Law School in 1969 which is no slouch in its own right having been founded over 140 years ago on the Notre Dame campus in South Bend, Indiana.

At Notre Dame we had one of the great university presidents of that era, Father Theodore Hesburgh, who served in that post for 35 years.[1] He was so respected nationally that it has been reported that he was even considered as a running mate for George McGovern in the 1972 presidential election.[2] We were also unusually fortunate to have a legendary law school dean, Joseph O'Meara, who put academic excellence over the coddling of any law student. In speaking of O'Meara in his memoir, Hesburgh recounts how O'Meara was responsible for making the law school a formidable academic institution after he took over in the early 1950s. "O'Meara's no-nonsense approach caused a furor. He felt that too many students were not serious about law and were not working hard enough. So out they went. He expelled half the students in the school, those who already had flunked one or more courses, including two sons of a Notre Dame professor.... More flunked out shortly after O'Meara took over. He wasted no time in tightening up everything: entrance requirements, curriculum, exams, and new standards for academic performance."[3]

Suffice it to say, Dean O'Meara will go down in the memory of all of us who were part of the O'Meara era at the Notre Dame Law School. He made us all better lawyers. And you can be assured that O'Meara would not have put up with disruptive law students regardless of what they wanted to protest. Nor would he have supported sycophantic professors taking long walks with first-year law students to discuss lofty issues - as Tribe did with Obama - in place of that student doing the basic legal research that all law students should do early in their law school experience. A law student understands and appreciates the importance to our democratic way of life of binding rules and precedent - or in other words, the importance of the Rule of Law - from hours of case study and research and not through long walks along the "Charles River" with ideologically preoccupied law professors.

And to make sure that the entire Notre Dame campus was first and foremost a place of higher learning, Hesburgh enforced his own version of the Rule of Law on campus to the ultimate benefit of all the students. So when Columbia University and the other so-called elite universities were exploding with turmoil in the 1960s, at Notre Dame Father Hesburgh succeeded in keeping a lid on this great university so that we could focus on the law and its principles instead dreaming up new theories to undermine the rule of law. I went to classes at Notre Dame in those troublesome days in the U.S. undisturbed and under the inspiring arms of "Touchdown Jesus" as he is affectionately called by Notre Dame students. This mural of Jesus - with outstretched arms on the library wall - can be seen from much of the campus, especially from the football stadium on game day.

In his memoir *God, Country, Notre Dame*, Father Hesburgh poignantly described the environment we lived through in the U.S. in those years at Notre Dame and on other campuses. "The high idealism, vigor, and youthful hopes that marked the inauguration of John F. Kennedy in 1961 ended in disillusion, anger and finally violence when the 1960s came to an end .... Proclaiming their distrust of everyone over thirty, they [students] fled parental authority, wore ragged clothing, used foul language, turned to mind altering drugs, disdained the work ethic, family and marriage, and more - all to find a new meaning and a new way to live their lives. When they wanted to voice their protests, they struck out, of course, at what was nearest to them: the colleges and universities from Berkeley in San Francisco to Columbia in New York City ...."[4]

Father Hesburgh was no right-wing conservative. Many of his accomplishments included being instrumental in starting the Peace Corps in the Kennedy administration in the early 1960s and serving as a member - and eventually as the chairman - of the U.S. Commission on Civil Rights from 1957–1972.[5] But notwithstanding this obvious liberal bent, he did not shirk from his leadership role which he recounted in his memoir. "At Columbia, students took over the office of the university's ill-fated president, Grayson Kirk. After they barricaded themselves inside, they proceeded to ransack his files, drink his sherry, smoke his cigars, and defecate on his rug. Similar outrages were carried out against several others among my colleagues of that time ...."[6]

Hesburgh's office was never taken over but he did face several challenges to his authority and campus life that many of us on campus were not even aware of. In successfully facing one threat to burn down the ROTC building on campus he, unlike many other university administrators of his day, met their protests with a mix of sensitivity and principles grounded in wisdom and courage. He recounts one talk he gave to a "throng of about two thousand students" who had gathered on the "main mall on campus .... Basically, I told the students that like them I was against the war in Vietnam, but unlike them, I was in favor of ROTC on campuses. Why? Because as long as nations needed armies, I believed the United States should have the best Army possible, run by the best people possible, and that meant the Army having people who had studied philosophy, theology and other humanities in our colleges and universities. Ideally, all military officers would possess this kind of education. In the best of all worlds, of course there would be no wars, no need for a military, but we had not yet reached that point."[7]

While the threat to burn down the ROTC building passed, things got worse as "students nationwide became more objectionable and violent ...." Because Notre Dame "seemed to be consumed in controversy..."as well, he determined the "time had come to draw the line."[8]

In a February, 1969 letter sent to all students, faculty, administrators and trustees, which I still remember reading as a law student, Hesburgh set forth what could be said to be an endearing example of what the Rule of Law is and what it can accomplish to save a "community." Unlike the Harvard CRITS who believed that the Rule of Law had to be destroyed before a utopian "community" would take its place, Hesburgh's letter showed the U.S. academic community - even if was too late for many of them - what a courageous, principled rule of law based stand could accomplish.

As he indicated in his memoir, "[s]omehow this letter touched a nerve. It was the first of its kind from a university president, the first firm drawing of the line on student protests, and it was widely taken as a blueprint of sorts for other colleges and universities …. [W]ithin two days of being sent to the students, the letter was reported in every newspaper in the country. The *New York Times* carried the full text."[9] Whether Father Hesburgh knew it at the time, there is little question that the letter and the law it established contained the historically important attributes of the Rule of Law - generality, certainty and equality of application. That is, it applied to all students generally --without establishing any exceptions --and the sanctions for violation were "certain" and clearly set forth. There wasn't even the faint hint of amnesty for some preferred group or individual. Nor did it require future regulations to be issued over months or years by campus bureaucrats who could exercise discretion and determine who would stay and who would be expelled. And as will become evident, it was enforced and applied impartially to all the violators. If only our current government officials and judges could have such wisdom and objectivity in drafting and enforcing laws.

In the excerpts that follow, while he recognized the right to protest grievances, his letter emphasized basic rule of law principles that should still ring true today.

"[V]iolation of others' rights and obstruction of the life of the university are outlawed as illegitimate means of dissent in this kind of open society. Violence is especially deplored as a violation of everything that the university community stands for.

"Now comes my duty of stating, clearly and unequivocally, what happens if…. [A]nyone or group that substitutes force for rational persuasion, be it violent or nonviolent, will be given fifteen minutes of meditation to cease and desist.... If they do not within that time period cease and desist, they will be asked for their identity cards. Those who produce them will be suspended from this community as not understanding what this community is. Those who do not have or will not produce identity cards will be assumed not to be members of this community and will be charged with trespassing...and treated accordingly by the law." Hesburgh's letter also addressed appeal rights both for students and faculty members so charged. But made clear that "[j]udgment of this matter will be delivered within five days following the facts, for justice delayed is justice denied to all concerned."[10]

As a lesson to all those who would dissolve the traditional understanding of the rule of law, as the CRITS - favored by Obama and some of his other Harvard classmates - hoped for, Hesburgh's words are telling: "There seems to be a current myth that university members are not responsible to the law, and that somehow the law is the enemy, particularly those whom society has constituted to uphold and enforce the law. I would like to insist here that all of us are responsible to the duly constituted laws of the university community and of the land. There is no other guarantee of civilization versus the jungle or mob rule, here or elsewhere. If someone invades your home, do you dialogue with him or call the law? Without the law, the university is a sitting duck for any small group from outside or inside that wishes to destroy it, to incapacitate it, to terrorize it at whim. The argument goes —or has gone —invoke the law and you lose the university community. *My only response is that without the law you may well lose the university - and beyond that - the larger society that supports it and that is most deeply wounded when law is no longer respected, bringing an end to everyone's most cherished rights .... Somewhere a stand must be made.*"[11] (emphasis supplied).

Hesburgh regretted that he was viewed as a "hawk" around the country as a result of his letter and actually opposed any possible federal legislation from the Nixon administration that would clamp down on campus disturbances. But that did not deter Hesburgh from enforcing the expulsion policy set forth in his February 1969 letter. About nine months after the letter was distributed a number of students were expelled following the rules set out in the letter for lying down in front of the placement office door thus blocking the entrance to the office on campus in which the CIA and Dow Chemical were conducting recruiting interviews of Notre Dame students. As Hesburgh indicated, "[t]hey demanded and received a hearing, but the rules were clear and they were out. All of those suspended returned the next semester and went on to graduation. And that was the end of the challenge to the university's right and ability to govern its students."[12]

We can't turn back the clock to the 1960s to install more courageous and farsighted leaders like Father Hesburgh on university campuses with the hope that they might possibly have blunted somewhat the movement of U.S. society away from traditional values and ideals such as the rule of law. But we can learn from his principled rule of law based approach to what Hesburgh called the "student revolution" of the 1960s that saved Notre Dame from the terrible fate that occurred on other campuses in that era. As he said in 1969 - words that are timeless and in my view applicable to the crumbling nature of the Rule of Law in the 21st century - "[m]y only response is that without the law you may well lose the university - and beyond that - the larger society that supports it and that is most deeply wounded when law is no longer respected, bringing an end to everyone's most cherished rights …. Somewhere a stand must be made."[13]

CHAPTER 7

The Battle for the Hearts and Minds of the Supreme Court

The tumultuous 1960s struck the Supreme Court just like the rest of American society. In the '60s, traditional values were hard to find and the Supreme Court had little problem inserting itself in the vacuum. This was the heyday of what came to be known as the "Warren Court." Chief Justice Earl Warren presided over the court from 1953–1969. And before he was through, the rule of law ideal that "laws and not men govern" would hardly be recognizable. As a Warren biographer, Jim Newton, aptly noted, "By the time he was through, Warren influenced his times more than any president with whom he served…. Today America is in many ways the America that Earl Warren made."[1] While this may be an accurate statement, there seems to be little doubt that he accomplished this feat functioning more like an unrestrained monarch than a judge in a constitutionally bound democracy who has a solemn obligation to act in an objective, impartial manner in applying the law as written.

When Warren was appointed Chief Justice of the Supreme Court in 1953 by President Dwight Eisenhower, he had had a noteworthy political career as a three-term governor of California and as the vice presidential candidate on the 1948 Republican ticket with Thomas Dewey, the unsuccessful challenger to President Harry Truman. Warren "never served a day as a judge" before becoming Chief Judge of the Court.[2] And it should have been no surprise that his style of judging has been characterized as "reliance on his own instincts for society's well-being."[3] This instinctual approach to the law - as opposed to rule of law oriented deference to precedent or as lawyers call it, *stare decisis* - is obvious when we consider that the Warren Court overturned more precedents than any other court in history – 33 precedents from

1963-69 alone. In the entire history of the Supreme Court up until that time, only eighty eight had been overturned.[4] One leading authority in the field has commented - in emphasizing the lack of a constitutional basis for its decisions - that for "two decades [the] Supreme Court pull[ed]one after another unanticipated finding in whole cloth out of the Constitution."[5]

President Eisenhower's disappointment in the unconstrained way Earl Warren acted as Chief Justice of the Supreme Court was clearly registered in his comments to Ronald Reagan. As Reagan recounted, "Dwight Eisenhower once told me that the biggest mistake he had made as president was appointing Earl Warren as Chief Justice of the Supreme Court because, in Ike's view, Warren had changed stripes and turned into a liberal who took it upon himself to rewrite the Constitution."[6]

Whether you believed his court's rulings were for "society's well-being" or not in the 1960s clearly depended on your sense of what kind of society and values you thought right for America. If you were on the right you supported "billboards proclaiming 'Impeach Earl Warren' [that] would dot the nation's highways."[7] If you were on the left, you applauded when Warren showed a "daring willingness to challenge social norms."[8] And you were giddy when Warren's six- member majority on the court struck down as unconstitutional a short, voluntary prayer in the New York schools which read in its entirety: "Almighty God, we acknowledge our dependence upon Thee, and we beg Thy blessings upon us, our parents, our teachers and our country."[9] And you thought this country was on the right track when the court "increased protection for pornography ... and found a constitutional right to privacy, notwithstanding [in Professor Tamanaha's words] that it was nowhere stated in the document."[10] This so-called "right to privacy" would become historic a few years later when it formed the foundational principle for the 1973 abortion case of *Roe v. Wade*.[11] Police departments all over the country were also stunned when the Warren Court issued its now famous, or infamous depending on your point of view, 1966 *Miranda* warning decision. This decision guaranteed all suspects the right to a lawyer and ushered in the age of defendants "lawyering up" to thwart police investigators as some would claim.[12]

The issue from a rule of law standpoint is not whether many of the Warren Court's decisions were bad or good in their own right but whether in a constitutional democracy, where the separation of powers is a bedrock principle, should unelected judges be making value judgments and establishing procedures and rules for police and citizens to follow instead of Congress or state legislatures? In this regard, summing up the objections of the minority on the Supreme Court - and many of the Warren Court's public critics who still believed that the law should be discovered and not made out of "whole cloth" to serve one's personal preferences - Justice John Marshall Harlan proclaimed in a 1969 dissenting opinion, "it [the decision] reflects to an unusual degree the current notion that this court possesses a peculiar wisdom all its own whose capacity to lead this country out of its present troubles is constrained only by the limits of judicial ingenuity in contriving new constitutional principles to meet each new problem as it arises."[13]

But it was after Warren's retirement that the blockbuster *Roe v. Wade* abortion decision would rock our world, in 1973, setting off a national schism that colors America's view of the Supreme Court and its justices to this day. In *Roe*, Warren's legacy lived on as the Supreme Court built on the Warren Court's precedents to establish new constitutional rules applicable to abortions that up to this time had been regulated by state laws. As the right to life and the pro-choice factions know so well, the court found that the "right to privacy … is broad enough to encompass a woman's decision to terminate her pregnancy."[14] And because the *Roe* case would depend on the woman's constitutional "right to privacy" first enunciated by the Warren Court in the 1965 *Griswold* case, "Griswold would be embroiled in America's exhausting, vicious abortion debate. It came to stand" [in Warren's biographer's words] "as a symbol of the Warren court's adventurism in the field of constitutional interpretation."[15]

As the opponents of *Roe* would argue, the Supreme Court far exceeded its judicial role and threw the "separation of powers" doctrine out the window when it struck down state statutes that made abortions illegal. The justices of the court stepping in the shoes of a state legislature established "trimester" criteria that allowed states to regulate abortions in greater degrees as the fetus developed in the womb.[16] It has been described as the "watershed event of contemporary Supreme Court history …. It was unlike any constitutional opinion ever written. For opponents, *Roe* reigns as the unmatched example of judicial arrogation of legislative power, of justices imposing their personal views on the populace in the name of interpreting the Constitution."[17]

After the *Roe* decision, a new battleground developed in this country as various interest groups began the long and now constant fight to seat Supreme Court justices they hope will share their ideological beliefs. In the process, the Rule of Law has been pushed to the side. The Supreme Court in Tamanaha's words would "become a target of specific groups with an overarching aim in mind. Seat individuals who share their particular agenda in order that their views can become the law. This is the effort to stock judicial positions as the key strategy for seizing the law to instrumentally further one's agenda."[18] In commenting on this battle over Supreme Court nominees in contemporary times, the eminent former federal judge and attorney general of the United States, Michael Mukasey, has written that it has existed "in the past few decades, certainly since the superbly qualified Robert Bork was turned down for a seat on the Supreme Court. The selection of judges has become a high stakes exercise for agenda-driven politics, with nominees often selected with at least one eye focused on their expected tilt on the issues of the day."[19]

Recall from Chapter 1 that Obama's mentor, Laurence Tribe, was the star witness for then Senator Joe Biden's Judiciary Committee's 1987 hearing in which Bork was pilloried. And what many may not know is that he played a role in the 2009 nomination of another one of his former Harvard Law School students, Elena Kagan, to the Supreme Court. In a surprisingly frank letter to Obama dated May 4, 2009 that I discovered while conducting research for this book we get a glimpse of the underlying motivations and machinations of those on the left as they scheme to place ideologically driven candidates on the Supreme Court. Obviously, Tribe hoped that this "leaked" letter would not become public.[20] His letter to Obama - replete with euphemisms or code words such as "humane," "pragmatic" and "progressive" to cover a liberal legal agenda - alarmingly goes beyond just discussing candidates to the court. Tribe highlights a much broader interest that he shares with his old student Obama. That is, reshaping the Rule of Law as we know it through the new "public face" of the Supreme Court - Elena Kagan. He even asks for a "newly created DOJ [Department of Justice] position for himself dealing with the rule of law." Obama subsequently gave Tribe a newly created position in his administration at the DOJ, as the "senior counselor for access to justice."[21]

Tribe's purposes for writing the letter are clear. With his former student in the White House, he saw an opportunity in his words to "lay the groundwork for a series of appointments [to the Supreme Court] that will gradually move the Court in a pragmatically, progressive direction."[22] The translation of which would go something like we want to put people on the court who are leftist in ideology and do not believe in the necessity to follow the Rule of Law. And in Tribe's view, the best way to accomplish this objective is for Obama to appoint Elena Kagan to the Supreme Court. As we all know, Obama did appoint Elena Kagan to the court in 2010.

Once on the bench, Tribe believes that because of Kagan's so-called "brilliance" and "political skill" she will be in a better position than others to "purchase"… "Tony Kennedy's mind." In Tribe's view, she would also be able to use her skills and "techniques" on other conservative justices –Samuel Alito, Antonin Scalia and John Roberts - "to see things her way." Justice Kennedy's "mind," in particular, is important to Tribe - and I'm sure to his former student Obama as well - because Kennedy is often the swing vote on close cases. But it would seem from the Supreme Court's June 28, 2012 decision in which Chief Justice Robert's joined Kagan and the other liberals on the Court to uphold the Obama Care individual mandate that Kagan was able to get Roberts to "see things her way." She obviously failed to "purchase" Kennedy's mind because he wrote the dissenting opinion supporting the invalidation of all of Obama Care. A "purchase" that he disappointingly confides to Obama that two other liberals on the court - Justices Breyer and Ruth Bader Ginsburg - have not been able to make. When we decode Tribe's semantics we find that he seems to be saying that Kagan will do a better job in either owning Justice Kennedy's "mind," or to take it a step further, that she will do a better job of brainwashing him so as to prevent him - in Tribe's language - from "drifting in a direction that is both formalistic and right-leaning …."[23] (From Justice Kennedy's tough questions to the government's lawyer during the Supreme Court arguments on Obama Care in late March 2012, it should have been clear that Elena Kagan had not been successful in "purchasing" the mind and independent spirit of Justice Kennedy. Disappointingly, though, such a disgusting Machiavellian plan hatched by Obama's former professor and hidden from the public until his 2009 letter to Obama was leaked may have had some success with Justice Roberts. Only time will tell if the "purchase" is permanent.) When Tribe uses the word "formalistic" what he is really saying is that Kennedy might drift toward the rule of law approach to decision-making basing his decision on the law as it is presented to him as opposed to an "ends justifies the means" approach endorsed by the left-leaning so-called "pragmatists" on the court. As we have seen, it appears that Chief Justice Roberts may have a new found interest in the Tribe inspired "ends justifies the means" approach.

Next and possibly what should concern all Americans is that Tribe's approach would allow judges to eat away at our rule of law inheritance even more in the future. Tribe urged Obama's appointment of Kagan because he believes she could make a real difference as the "public face of the Supreme Court" to advance a more "humane ... conception of the rule of law and the role of courts in the pursuit of justice."[24] In my experience, the insertion of the word "humane" to condition the rule of law ideal is code for allowing judges to act arbitrarily on their emotions or personal preferences when administering justice, instead of following the law as written.

Obama obviously agrees with Tribe's view. He has said in public comments that justices he nominates for a seat on the Supreme Court should act with "empathy" when deciding cases. This is just another euphemism to give cover to judges who arbitrarily decide cases based on considerations outside of the law. While words like "empathy" and "humane" sound good, they have tragic consequences for the Rule of Law and all those who plan their lives on the long-term stability and predictability of the rule of law attributes of "certainty," "equality of application" and "generality," that the law should guarantee. In Obama's own words "justice" isn't about the judge faithfully following the law, as shocking as that may sound! In unequivocal terms he would have judges build into their "decisions" and "outcomes"– nebulous and subjective concepts that spell tyranny by judges and their political masters.

"I will seek someone who understands that justice isn't about some abstract legal theory or footnote in a casebook; it is also about how our laws affect the daily realities of people's lives, whether they can make a living and care for their families, whether they feel safe in their homes and welcome in their own nation....I view that quality of *empathy*, of understanding and identifying with people's hopes and struggles, *as an essential ingredient* for arriving at *just decisions* and *outcomes*."[25]

Instead of judges following the law, that is, the "abstract legal theory" that applies "generally" to all people and gives everyone the same equal and predictable opportunity, Obama - like Tribe - wants judges to lean on the scales of justice to tip them one way or another. In Obama's way of thinking, justice should no longer be blind. Judges, on the other hand, in determining the outcome of cases, should "identify with people's hopes and struggles," consider the "daily realities of people's lives" and whether they are "welcome in their own nation." Because someone must exercise discretion and pick one litigant over another based on these extra legal, fuzzy considerations - largely influenced by the judges' prejudices and passions - our U.S. legal system would no longer be recognizable to our founders. Sadly, under this discriminatory and arbitrary way of judging, it could no longer be said that we live in a society where we have a "government of laws and not men" and tyranny is not far off. Under Obama's concept of a legal system, a constitutional principle or the wording of a statute that the working man, retiree or businessman may have spent their lives relying on to create their life savings or the foundation of a successful business could be trumped by a judge who identified more with the "hopes and struggles" of one litigant over another.[26]

And the idea that judges who follow the rule of law are "inhumane" as Tribe would have us believe is insulting to our legal system and nothing more than a clever semantic trick that I've seen often used by trial lawyers in litigation. They characterize the opposition or its argument in a way that has little resemblance to the truth to evoke anger and revulsion so as to sway a gullible jury. Tribe does the same thing in his letter probably to give cover to himself and Obama in the off chance his letter became public. The truth is that the rule of law ideal that emphasizes "certainty" and "equality of application" could not be more humane. It has been the bedrock of this nation's constitutional democracy since the 18th century and without it we would not have thrived economically, benefitting everyone from the factory floor to the front office. And without this rich rule of law heritage, we could have become nothing more than a tyrannical and inhuman thug of a country a long time ago.

Tribe went on to point out in his 2009 letter to Obama that Earl Warren was one of the few Supreme Court justices in the past whose "public face" made a difference and that apparently Tribe believes

Kagan, like Warren before her "would project a well-grounded image of justice as fairness and of the law as codified common sense." If we stop again for a moment to translate what Tribe is saying, he is highlighting for Obama that Warren was successful - at least among liberals - in marketing to the public his re-write of the Constitution on the basis of such nebulous, subjective concepts as "fairness" and "common sense."And that Kagan as a "public face" of the Supreme Court and a skillful politician would do a Warren-like job of marketing her so-called "progressive" agenda that Tribe points out later in the letter is shared by Obama as well.[27]

Tribe also makes sure that Obama realizes that Kagan "would be a much more formidable match for Justice Scalia than Justice Breyer has been … in the kinds of public settings in which it has been all too easy for Scalia to make his rigid and unrealistic formalism seem synonymous with the rule of law and to make Breyer's pragmatism seem mushy and unconstrained by comparison."[28] The reason Tribe singles out Scalia and Breyer is because they represent the competing judicial philosophies that are currently present in the so-called liberal and conservative wings of the Supreme Court. And there is little doubt that Tribe hopes Kagan can do a better job than Breyer of marketing the liberal "unconstrained" approach to the rule of law.

Scalia's judicial philosophy is rule-bound or, in other words, based on historically established rule of law principles. Under Scalia's approach, a judge's discretion is constrained so that he or she cannot roam around to determine the "ends" to be achieved and then work backwards to manipulate his or her interpretation or the means to justify the preconceived ends. He calls himself a "textualist" in that he bases his interpretation of the Constitution and statutes on the text of the document. And he believes that those who depart from the "text" of the document can then engage in "free-wheeling lawmaking." (Chief Roberts became a "free-wheeling" lawmaker when he rewrote the text of Obama Care to call a "penalty" a "tax" to save the Act.) In lectures that were published in 1997, Justice Scalia directly rebuts Tribe's criticism of his judicial philosophy and shows clearly that Tribe's 2009 comments to Obama are really an attack on the rule of law. "Of all the criticism leveled against textualism, the most mindless is that it is 'formalistic." The answer to that is, of course it's formalistic. The rule of law is about form ...long live formalism. It is what makes a government a government of laws and not men."[29]

Breyer's decision-making philosophy, on the other hand, would allow judges the discretion to pick winners and losers - based on factors apart from the document to be interpreted. In Breyer's own words from his book entitled *Active Liberty*, Breyer concedes that in order to resolve "contemporary problems of government through law" he takes it upon himself to supplement "ordinary, judicial approaches."[30] Unfortunately for the Rule of Law, this is the philosophy that Chief Justice Roberts and the other liberals on the Supreme Court adopted in upholding the individual mandate in Obama Care. They were ready, willing and able to ignore their "solemn obligation" to the Rule of Law and supplement "ordinary judicial approaches" to solve what in their minds was a "contemporary problem" by simply rewriting the law. This rule of law end run was not lost on the rule of law oriented dissenters, Justices Kennedy, Scalia, Alito and Thomas. The following passages from the dissenting opinion highlight the flimsy basis for Chief Justice Roberts' decision:

"The issue is not whether Congress had the power to frame the minimum-coverage provision as a tax, but whether it did so...."

"But we cannot rewrite the statute to be what it is not. '"[A]lthough this Court will often strain to construe legislation so as to save it against constitutional attack, it must not and will not carry this to the point of perverting the purpose of a statute ... or judicially rewriting it.'"

"Our cases establish a clear line between a tax and a penalty: '[A] tax is an enforced contribution to provide for the support of the government; a penalty ... is an exaction imposed by statute as punishment for an unlawful act.'"

"Against the mountain of evidence that the minimum coverage requirement is what the statute calls it - a requirement - and that the penalty for its violation is what the statute calls it - a penalty - the Government brings forward the flimsiest of indications to the contrary."

"For all these reasons, to say that the Individual Mandate merely imposes a tax is not to interpret the statute but to rewrite it."

"We have no doubt that Congress knew precisely what it was doing when it rejected an earlier version of this legislation that imposed a tax instead of a requirement-with-penalty .... Imposing a tax through judicial legislation inverts the constitutional scheme, and places the power to tax in the branch of government least accountable to the citizenry."

"But we never—*never*—treated as a tax an exaction which faces up to the critical difference between a tax and a penalty, and explicitly denominates the exaction a 'penalty.' Eighteen times in 5000A [the individual mandate section] and elsewhere throughout the Act, Congress called the exaction … a 'penalty.'"

'What counts is what the statute says, and that is entirely clear."[31]

Contrary to the approach taken by the dissenters in the Obama Care case, Breyer's approach to decision-making clearly ignores the Rule of Law. It involves going beyond the text of the Constitution or a statute to find its "purpose" by looking to its "consequences, including 'contemporary conditions, social, industrial and political of the community to be affected.'"[32] Breyer even concedes that his decision-making philosophy - which it could be contended undergirds the decision-making approach of all of the liberal faction of the court, i.e., Justices Breyer, Ginsburg, Sotomayor and Kagan and for the Obama Care case, Justice Roberts too, - cannot meet the critical rule of law goals of predictability and stability. In this connection, Breyer acknowledges the human need "to plan in reliance upon the law [and] the need for predictability [and] for stability." But admits his approach could "leave the court without a clear rule" [and] a court focused on consequences may decide a case in a way that radically changes the law."[33] He tells us, though, not to worry about the absence of the rule of law objectives of "predictability" and stability" in his decisions - presumably by the other liberal justices as well - because a judge following his "purposive" judicial philosophy will not go off the wagon very often inasmuch as over time the judge "constrains [his] subjectivity."[34]

What is clear is that Justice Breyer's decision-making philosophy is antithetical to the historical role of judges in our country - going back to its founding and continuing to this day - in the minds of those who stillsee the role of judges as a "solemn obligation." It appears, though, the good professor Tribe believes his former student Elena Kagan will do a better job overcoming this fundamental, democratic roadblock than the "mushy [and] unconstrained" Breyer.

Regardless of Tribe's views, history is clear. Alexander Hamilton couldn't have been more emphatic on the importance of judges adhering to the rule of law: "To avoid an arbitrary discretion in courts, it is indispensable that they should be bound down by strict rules and precedent, which serve to define and point out their duty in every particular case that comes before them."[35] And Hamilton's admonitions were reinforced about 40 years later by one of this country's earliest and most renowned Chief Justices of the Supreme Court, John Marshall, when he proclaimed "Courts are mere instruments of law, and can will nothing."[36] Moving to the 20th century, Hayek emphasizes in his epic work *The Constitution of Liberty* - a treatise that Margaret Thatcher lived by - why judges should not have the discretion to pick winners by departing from the law as written: "And it is because the judge who apples them [laws] has no choice in drawing the conclusions that follow from the existing body of rules and the particular facts of the case, that it can be said that laws and not men govern."[37]

And the reasons why judges must follow strict rules when deciding cases are as valid today as they were when Aristotle warned about the "passions" of government officials over two millennia ago. As professor Tamanaha, tells us "[w]hen … ignorance, weakness, subconscious bias, corruption, and the desire for power are admitted as natural human traits, the possibility that rule by law may become rule by judges is no longer a benign possibility but a matter of real concern."[38] In my judgment, given the lengths that Chief Justice Roberts and the liberal faction of the Court went to rewrite Obama Care, there is little question that the human traits of "weakness" in the face of pressure and "bias" played key roles in the Supreme Court substituting the Rule of Law for their "rule by judges." Since Congress and Obama could not bring forth a law that meets constitutional requirements, five Supreme Court Justices simply rewrote it for them so that the massive government takeover of health care could become a reality. Constitutional law scholar, Dr. John Eastman, Professor of Law at the Chapman University School of Law and Director of the Center for Constitutional Jurisprudence at the Claremont Institute had this to say about the Supreme Court's Obama Care ruling: "The opinion by Chief Justice Roberts upholding the Affordable Care Act (aka Obamacare) as a valid exercise of Congress's taxing power is a sell-out of constitutional principle of the first magnitude…. It is also fundamentally wrong on constitutional law; the doctrine of separation of powers; the meaning of a direct tax; and the idea of limited government and enumerated powers."[39]

The *Wall Street Journal* summed up this disappointing state of affairs for the Rule of Law and our constitutionally based political system by concluding that "Chief Justice Roberts's ruling is careless about these bedrock tax questions ... His ruling, with its multiple contradictions and inconsistencies, reads as if it were written by someone affronted by the government's core constitutional claims, *but who wanted to uphold the law anyway to avoid political blowback and thus found a pretext for doing so in the taxing power ....* (Emphasis supplied) If this understanding is correct, then Chief Justice Roberts behaved like a politician, which is more corrosive to the rule of law and the court's legitimacy than any abuse it would have taken from a ruling that President Obama disliked .... But the Court's most important role is to protect liberty when the political branches exceed the Constitution's bounds, not to bless their excesses in the interests of political or personal expediency or both. On one of the most consequential cases he will ever hear, Chief Justice Roberts failed this most basic responsibility."[40]

While it is under siege, there is still hope that our historically revered Rule of Law is not an anachronism that will go the way of other values that were lost in the 1960s. In the 2006 Senate confirmation hearings in connection with his nomination to the Supreme Court, judge Alito echoed the sentiments of our founders and the great philosophers of the past when he testified that, "The judge's only obligation is to the rule of law. And what that means is that in every single case the judge has to do what the law requires."[41] There is little question, though, as we have seen earlier in this book, Obama's warnings to the conservative rule of law oriented justices against overturning his Obama Care mandate that were made shortly after the March 2012 arguments, was also a message to the Court. In Obama's world, Supreme Court justices must ignore their "solemn obligation" to the law and follow instead the "natural human traits" of "bias" and "weakness." This, in the end, is the only way he can move this country to a "government of men and women," namely himself, some unelected bureaucrats and a few Supreme Court justices who unquestionably accept his world view.

But even if Justice Roberts' departure from rule of law principles is temporary, the hope that justices will follow the Rule of Law and not their personal preferences, may not be long lasting if, in a second term, Obama gets to replace just one of the more conservative justices - Kennedy, Scalia, Thomas, or Alito. Remember, Supreme Court justices are appointed for life. And as history teaches, the unelected Warren Court set new values for the American public with less godliness, more pornography and as many would claim the handcuffing of the police. A liberal majority that respects its own personal preferences or in Tribe's terms being "humane" or, in Obama's view, making "empathy" a key decision-making ingredient - more than the impartiality and objectivity demanded by the Rule of Law - spells less certainty and stability for our economy and less individual freedom. And it also spells more values- based decisions from Supreme Court justices pulled out of thin air and inserted into the Constitution that may make the terms "family or Judeo-Christian values" seem as anachronistic as a rotary telephone.

CHAPTER 8

REDISTRIBUTE WEALTH AGENDA, JOE THE PLUMBER & THE IRON LADY

When Obama answered a question at an October 2008 campaign stop asked by Joe Wurzelbacher, an Ohio plumber - with his now famous comment that we need to "spread the wealth around"- he was not only making Joe the Plumber a household name, but was also telling the world what he thought about the Rule of Law.[1] Joe the Plumber would become a favorite of the media because of his straight-forward, unembellished reaction to then candidate Obama's Freudian slip. Obama's "spread the wealth around" comment would also become a campaign target for the McCain-Palin campaign. Unfortunately, like so many other campaign themes, it was swept aside by the tide of bad economic news in the fall of 2008 that helped propel Obama to the White House.

But when we look back at his comment in hindsight, with the knowledge gained from observing Obama's performance over the last four years and evaluating his record in office, it becomes clear that he is doing his utmost to fulfill the governing philosophy he expressed to Joe the Plumber. The daily drumbeat from the president that those making more than $250,000 a year should pay more in taxes because they are not paying their "fair share" - while about half of American households do not pay any federal income taxes at all - is a prime example of the "wealth redistributionist" agenda in President Obama's view of the welfare state.[2] When we cut through it, his Joe the Plumber comment is just one more piece of evidence that reveals his disdain for the Rule of Law.

We can never lose sight of the cold, hard reality that in order to take from one person or class and give to another, in other words to "redistribute wealth" that government officials have to "pick winners and losers." Remember that when the government does not follow general rules that apply equally to everyone in a certain, predictable way, as enshrined in the rule of law ideal, and dictates winners and losers instead through the exercise of their discretion, it can no longer be said that "laws and not men" govern society. These so-called enlightened rulers accomplish their objective through welfare state legislation and elaborate administrative agency "planning" schemes that usually take the form of regulations or agency enforcement actions that seek goals such as "distributive justice" or "environmental sustainability."

The penalty we all pay for this governmental intrusion has been cogently summarized in a thoughtful, contemporary analysis of the Rule of Law in a welfare state setting by Bill Scheuerman in *Politics and Society*. "Evidence continues to mount that crucial components of the rule of law are disintegrating under the conditions of the contemporary regulatory state.... If a minimal demand of the rule of law was always that state action should take predictable form contemporary democracies do poorly in living up to this standard."[3]

One has to look no further than the current American economy for glaring and sad examples of the damage caused when a society fails to adhere to the rule of law ideal and instead becomes enamored with "social justice" ends and regulatory overreach. As *CNN Money* tells us, nearly 13 million people are out of work.[4] And we have a rotting housing market - in which nearly 15 million homeowners have lost so much value in their homes that they can't afford to sell and buy another home. As reported by CNBC late last year, "It's as if one half of potential buyers in America died over a two year period."[5] There is little question that this sickness was largely caused by governmental social engineering schemes. These welfare state programs stimulated a devastating housing bubble and the Obama administration housing relief programs over the last four years suffer from many of the same infirmities.

Decades ago, F.A. Hayek concluded that the concept of so-called distributive justice is not compatible with the Rule of Law and "bluntly" uncovered for us what it is really based upon. And in applying that wisdom to our housing market collapse, we find that in forcing some banks and encouraging others to make mortgage loans available to those who could not afford them, government officials violated one of the foundational principles of the Rule of Law. That is, the "basic postulate of a free society" is that laws apply equally to all. When the government seeks - through social engineering - to artificially rig the housing market to accomplish "social justice" objectives it hurts everyone, as the current housing market tragedy attests to. As Hayek tells us "economic inequality [does] not justify our resorting to discriminatory coercion or privilege as a remedy."[6]

The motivation for the housing market bubble, as well as other exercises in distributive justice that the Obama administration has made a key part of its governing philosophy, is clear. When you drill down to the root cause for welfare state, distributive justice schemes, Hayek found that it is the worst of all "anti-social ... passions"- "envy." Hayek minced no words. "When we inquire into the justification of these demands [for so-called social justice] we find that they rest on the discontent that the success of some people often produces in those that are less successful, or, to put it bluntly, on envy. The modern tendency to gratify this passion and to disguise it in the respectable garment of social justice is developing into a serious threat to individual freedom .... If all unfulfilled desires have a claim on the community, individual responsibility is at an end .... It is probably one of the essential conditions for the preservation of a ... [free] society that we do not countenance *envy*, not sanction its demands by camouflaging it as social justice, but treat it, in the words of John Stuart Mill, as 'the most anti-social and evil of all passions.'" (Emphasis supplied)[7]

As we have already seen in earlier chapters, Hayek was not just any run- of- the- mill professor and his teaching is as valuable today as it was decades ago. He received doctorates in law and political science in the 1920s from the University of Vienna and also studied philosophy, psychology and economics. He emigrated from Austria to England in 1931 and became "a naturalized British subject in 1938." He served as the Tooke Professor of Economic Science and Statistics at the London School of Economics from 1931–1950. He also taught for years at the University of Chicago.[8]

Beyond his writings on the Rule of Law and government, in 1974 he was awarded the Nobel Prize in economics. And his accolades keep coming in the 21st century. In 2011 his simple, yet brilliant article "The Use of Knowledge in Society" was highlighted as one of the top 20 articles in the first hundred years of the prestigious *American Economic Review*.[9] In his article, he showed that "central planning" in which government tries to control the economy from the top down (think Obama's Washington bureaucracy) is no match for "competition." Instead of trying to focus all relevant knowledge in a few minds, "competition" benefits from the enormous economic power of "knowledge that is dispersed among many people" that all moves in the "right direction" by simply following the movement of a few key "prices."[10]

Winston Churchill thought so much of Hayek's works that he read *The Road to Serfdom* on the eve of the 1945 election, shortly after it was published in London.[11] Margaret Thatcher, the renowned British prime minister from 1979–1990, was an unabashed follower of his teachings. She thought so much of his contributions to free enterprise economics that she was instrumental in seeing that he was honored in 1984 by Queen Elizabeth II of England for his "services to the study of economics."[12]

In fact, she was such a staunch believer of Hayek's writings that according to John Ranelagh, author of *Thatcher's People*, at a summer 1975 meeting of the Conservative Party's Research Department in which a speaker proposed that the "'middle way' was the pragmatic path for the Conservative Party to take, avoiding the extremes of the Left or Right, before he had finished speaking [she] reached into her briefcase and took out a book. It was … Hayek's *The Constitution of Liberty*. Interrupting our pragmatist, she held the book up for all of us to see. 'This', she said sternly, 'is what we believe,' and banged Hayek on the table."[13] Renelagh also reports that Thatcher "once described Hayek as one of the three great intellects of the twentieth century."[14]

It is no wonder that Thatcher integrated Hayek's teaching into her policies. She was very knowledgeable, inquisitive and perceptive - with degrees in chemistry and law from Oxford - and a firm believer in the free enterprise principles that Hayek demonstrated depended on the Rule of Law.[15] And she clearly understood and appreciated the wisdom in Hayek's multi-disciplinary approach. It has been said about Hayek that his "principal effort was to articulate a systematic view embracing many sciences and intellectual disciplines.[16]

Hayek was an extraordinary thinker. Like no other before or after him he brought economics, law and political philosophy together in such a manner that the keys to personal freedom and economic success were there for the taking for any politician willing and courageous enough to buck the welfare state trend and implement his teaching. A 21st century scholar has aptly characterized Hayek's economic and rule of law synergy; a synergy that Thatcher and Reagan well understood, as noted below, and that Obama and FDR ignored, thus resulting in catastrophic damage for all in society:

"Simply, the world is in a state of constant flux. Billions of economic transactions are conducted every minute throughout the world and it truly is a miracle that any productive economic activity happens, much less economic activity on such a great scale .... Add in the dynamic feature that all of these decisions are subject to a constant feedback loop as millions of individual purchasing decisions send signals about the relative demand for different products, and it is remarkable that the coordination occurs at all .... Hayek's profound [economic] observation is that the price system [and not intrusive government controls] is the mechanism by which this profound coordination occurs, leading to a functioning economy .... Hayek's corollary observation is that ... the goal of social and political institutions is to minimize the number of variables that threaten coordination." And that the "legal regime" in a society "might be the largest and most important variable." Thus, "Hayek's central insight about the value of the rule of law is that in a world defined by flux and dynamism, economic activity requires as much stability as possible from institutions like the legal regime ...."[17]

Hayek's great contributions to political philosophy and the Rule of Law -*The Constitution of Liberty*- published in 1960 and *The Road to Serfdom* published in 1944 - are listed in the top ten of the 100 best non-fiction books of the 20th century.[18] President Ronald Reagan also was a follower of Hayek.[19] As Martin Anderson, the author of *Revolution* says, Hayek was among the 2 or 3 people who most influenced his philosophy and Reagan welcomed Hayek to the White House as a special guest.[20] And in 1991 Hayek was awarded the Presidential Medal of Freedom, one of the two highest civilian awards in the U.S.[21]

The potential abuse of discretion by government bureaucrats which then becomes memorialized in the law was a principal concern of Hayek's writings. However, it does not seem to trouble the Obama administration. As Hayek explained, "[i]n the end somebody's views will have to decide whose interests are more important; and these views must become part of the law of the land, a new distinction of rank which the coercive apparatus of the government imposes upon people ...."[22] And if you think Hayek's concerns about the "coercive apparatus of the government" do not apply to 21st century America, think again. Just one of many regulatory actions of the Obama administration that stretched the objectivity and impartiality of the Rule of Law beyond recognition-- occurred in the fall of 2011. Obama's National Labor Relations Board in an unusually bold, partisan effort to pander to union special interests and to harass an employer who tried to do business in one of the right- to- work states coerced Boeing through a meritless unfair labor practice lawsuit. In reality, the objective of the arbitrary NLRB action was to force Boeing into making concessions to its union labor force in Washington State, before it would allow Boeing to open a plant in South Carolina, a right- to- work state.[23] Clearly this is a case of the NLRB virtually "commanding" Boeing to pay up to the Washington state unions - a form of regulatory extortion - before it allowed Boeing to do business in South Carolina. Boeing's unrestricted right to do business in South Carolina should never have been in question under the Rule of Law.

While written decades before the NLRB's arbitrary "ends justifies the means" approach to Boeing, Hayek stressed for us what the result should be in a government that respects the Rule of Law. "[U]nder the Rule of Law, government is prevented from stultifying individual efforts by *ad hoc* action …. Within the known rules of the game the individual is free to pursue his personal ends and desires, certain that the powers of government will not be used to frustrate his efforts." What we should be able to expect from our government operating under the Rule of Law and what the Obama administration's arbitrary actions demonstrate are obvious when we consider Hayek's example of the "general principle." "The difference between the two … is the same as that between laying down a Rule of the Road … and ordering people where to go; or … between providing signposts and ordering people which road to take."[24] There is little question that the Obama administration believes it has the power in the 21st century to tell U.S. citizens "what road to take" whether it involves Boeing, a car company's right to manufacture the cars of its choice, an individual's decision whether or not to buy health insurance or how to practice one's religion when it conflicts with the government's health care contraception mandates.

As Thatcher and Reagan well knew, Hayek opens our eyes to the economic and personal freedom graveyard we face if we do not renew our belief in the Rule of Law. As Hayek explained "It is no exaggeration to say that if we had to rely on conscious central planning for the growth of our industrial system, it would never have reached the degree of differentiation, complexity and flexibility it has attained …. [C]entral planning is incredibly clumsy, primitive and limited in scope."[25] And we should be mindful that while it may be harder to recognize the socialist-like policies of 21st century welfare state society, they are not far removed from their predecessors. As Hayek highlighted in the Preface to his 1976 edition of *The Road to Serfdom*, "socialism has come to mean chiefly the extensive redistribution of incomes through taxation and the institutions of the welfare state. In the latter kinds of socialism the effects … are brought about more slowly, indirectly, and imperfectly. I believe the ultimate outcome tends to be very much the same …."[26] And that outcome has been succinctly captured by a noted British author, George Orwell, of the mid 20th century: "Socialism necessarily gives power to an inner circle of bureaucrats who in almost every case will be men who want power for its own sake and will stick to nothing in order to retain it."[27]

As the *Wall Street Journal* points out, we need to look no further than our U.S. Medicare program for an example of a "clumsy" and "limited" program that has been "centrally planned from Washington" and in need of major reform. "The brutal math is that Medicare spending has been growing about three percentage points faster every year than the overall economy for the last quarter-century and is now the main driver of the fiscal crisis." But instead of accepting Hayek-like free market alternatives that would compete with the welfare state bureaucracy, "Mr. Obama has ruled out any structural reforms and his only fallback is the command-and-control technology that continues to fail and will ultimately harm patient care."[28]

And the link between the free-wheeling discretion exercised by bureaucrats and the demise of the Rule of Law was not limited to F.A. Hayek. There is little question that Obama's revolutionary Professor Unger well understood - at the time Obama enthusiastically participated in his Harvard classes - how the broad discretion exercised by bureaucrats who implement a welfare state policy can undermine the Rule of Law. As Unger explained in his anti-rule of law treatise, "[t]he quest for substantive [distributive] justice corrupts legal generality [treating everyone the same] …. No matter how substantive justice is defined, it can be achieved only by treating different situations differently.[29] In discussing the lengths that "distributive justice" can take,

Unger shines a light on affirmative action as another way to undermine the traditional rule of law ideal. He emphasizes that when government officials are focused on remedying "impermissible inequalities [they] may require a reverse preference to the disadvantaged group."[30] While both Hayek and Unger understood the potential damage that a government's "distributive justice" agenda could do to the Rule of Law, Unger and Hayek had different agendas in mind. Obama's professor and confidant Unger hoped for the demise of the Rule of Law, while Hayek sought to save it to advance the cause of freedom and economic well being of society.

Given Unger's understanding of the damage that the "distributive justice" agenda does to the rule of law ideal and Obama's awareness of it, it is clear that Obama recklessly or intentionally disregarded the truth of its harmful effects when he adopted his "spread the wealth" strategy to govern American society in the post-financial crisis times of 2009-2012. In this regard, we should not lose sight of Obama's reason for attending Harvard Law School. He hoped to obtain the "tools" to achieve his political agenda and there is little question that his Harvard professors –Unger and Tribe to name two - provided those tools.

So what can we learn from Thatcher - who followed Hayek's teaching and not the Professor Ungers of the world - that might apply directly to our 21st century economic crisis in the U.S. ? By way of background, as Charles Moore her official biographer tells us, Margaret Thatcher was "the first woman prime minister in the English speaking world and the longest- serving British prime minister of either sex since universal suffrage …. And she was dubbed "The Iron Lady" even before she was elected prime minister. After becoming leader of the Conservative Party in 1975, Mrs. Thatcher opened a new, controversial front in the Cold War with the Soviet Union." And because of her tough stance against Soviet communism the Soviet Army newspaper, Red Star, "christened her The Iron Lady."[31]

We lawyers look for precedents to solve problems and there is lot we can learn from the British other than how to throw a royal wedding. In short, Obama's disdain for the Rule of Law as evidenced by his wealth redistributionist governing philosophy and reliance on a burgeoning federal bureaucracy to pick the winners and losers was the same prescription for economic disaster that Britain's leftist politicians followed to ruin Britain's economy. In the 1970s, the British economy was reeling from an economic maelstrom largely caused by skyrocketing deficits, wealth redistributionist government policies and a weak currency - the very reasons many argue why the U.S. economy has struggled over the last few years and millions are out of work.

Instead of more wealth redistribution and regulations as urged by Obama, Prime Minister Thatcher, led Great Britain out of its economic wilderness with a much different philosophy. The Conservative Party's governing philosophy, in her words, was based on "limited government under a rule of law rather than ... the kind of state we must avoid - a socialist state where bureaucrats rule by discretion."[32] Not unlike Obama administration actions during his first term (for example, Stimulus, Obama Care and Dodd-Frank), designed to take advantage of the financial crisis of 2008, left-leaning British politicians seized an opportunity in the 1940s to benefit from the World War II crisis. They were successful after the war when the public turned wartime Conservative leader, Winston Churchill, out of office and began transforming Britain into a welfare state. This included sweeping legislation with national health insurance as part of the "social insurance" package. This so-called "social insurance" had been a key component of a wartime movement to change the face of Great Britain when the war ended.

According to Jose Harris, the biographer of the movement's WWII leader, William Beveridge, social insurance was only the "iceberg tip." He had a more far-reaching program of social reconstruction in mind including the nationalization of industries and permanent state control of incomes and prices.[33] This view of Utopia that the post-war Labor Party partially adopted over the years was paid for with a heavy reliance on Keynesian economic principles - in other words, massive government intervention into the economy and deficit spending. A quick look at the Obama administration's initiatives - including Obama Care, the Dodd-Frank law's efforts to dominate the banking industry and the virtual take-over of GM and Chrysler - tells all of us that he is trying to head down the same road taken by the British socialists, but to do it much faster, especially if he is elected to a second term.

After 30 years of big government programs, Britain hit rock bottom in 1976 and sought a bailout from the International Monetary Fund. By the mid-70s, its annual deficit-to-GDP ratio hovered around 9% (U.S. one year deficit of $1.3 trillion in 2011 hovers around 9% of our gross domestic product or GDP).[34] In 1979, the British people had had enough and turned to Margaret Thatcher and her Conservative Party to lead the country. As a 2008 retrospective in the *Daily Mail* highlights, though, Thatcher's rise was not easy. The establishment despised her; she became a TV joke line and was criticized as a "common provincial upstart."[35]

Notwithstanding the critics, Thatcher's understanding of Britain's economic problems and the intellectual basis for their solution was clear. As she tells us in her memoirs, books by F.A. Hayek were "right at the top of [her] reading list."[36] From Hayek's *The Road to Serfdom,* she was alerted to the profound harmful implications of intrusive government control and planning.[37] And from what she called Hayek's "masterpieces" – *The Constitution of Liberty and Law, Legislation and Liberty,* she "really came to think" of the Rule of Law principle as having a "wider application" than the narrow view of the principle she had learned studying law.[38] Her appreciation of the rule of law ideal would grow as she practiced law before entering British politics full time. "Studying, observing, discussing and eventually practicing law had a profound effect on my political outlook. In this, I was probably unusual. Familiarity with the law usually breeds if not contempt, at least a large measure of cynicism. For me, however, it gave a richer significance, to that expression 'rule of law' which so easily tripped off the Conservative tongue."[39]

In speaking of her beliefs relative to the hazards to our personal and economic wellbeing of centralized government planning and ultimately state socialism, Thatcher highlighted the wisdom of Winston Churchill and F.A. Hayek:

"In the end Churchill was right. Whether socialism needed a 'Gestapo' as it did in Eastern Europe and the Soviet Union, or just those banal and bureaucratic instruments of coercion, confiscatory taxation, nationalization and oppressive regulation employed in the West, ultimately depended only on the degree of socialism desired. In diminishing economic freedom, the socialists had embarked on a course which if pursued to its ultimate destination, would mean the extinction of all freedom. I had no doubt myself about the truth of such position .... Not surprisingly..., the most powerful critique of socialist planning and the socialist state which I read at this time, and to which I have returned so often since, F.A. Hayek's *The Road To*

Serfdom, is dedicated "to the Socialists of all parties …. At this stage it was the (to my mind) unanswerable criticisms of socialism in *The Road to Serfdom* which had an impact. Hayek saw that Nazism - National Socialism - had its roots in nineteenth-century German social planning. He showed that intervention by the state in one area of the economy or society gave rise to almost irresistible pressures to extend planning further into other sectors. He alerted us to the profound, indeed revolutionary implications of state planning for Western civilization as it had grown up over the centuries."[40]

In reflecting on the state of affairs in Great Britain when she became prime minister in 1979, a state of affairs that is clearly relevant to the misguided efforts of the Obama administration during its first four years in office, Thatcher tells us that the Labour Party (Britain's answer to our Democrats) had spent the years since WWII trying to "kick-start resurgence [with] a centralizing, managerial, bureaucratic, interventionist style of government … with high rates of tax on work [and] … wealth transfer…. It managed the economy … by Keynesian methods of fiscal manipulation …."[41] She went on to proclaim that "Keynesian economics … had underpinned Government policy since the war."[42] Without mincing words, she concluded "It gloried in … regulation, controls and subsidies….Yet it was a miserable failure in every respect."[43]

Like all politicians, Thatcher's policies were influenced by her formative years. In this regard, it is telling how different Thatcher's background was to that of our current president who relied on radical professors, Reverend Wright, a clergyman who used profanity to characterize America, and a former domestic terrorist for intellectual and religious support. As the daughter of a small-town grocer, Thatcher believed strongly in the virtue of personal responsibility. To Thatcher, "thrift was a virtue and profligacy a vice …."[44] She also believed that "one can never do without straight-forward commonsense in matters great as well as small."[45]

Her "intellectual religious formation" was largely impacted by the "religious writings" of the extraordinary mid 20th century author C.S. Lewis. To Thatcher, Lewis' *The Screwtape Letters* "convincingly" tells us how "evil works on our human weaknesses." And she found that no one has ever made "more accessible the profound concepts of Natural Law" than Lewis did in the "opening passages" of his extraordinary little book "Mere Christianity."[46] (I couldn't agree more.) Thatcher can also teach something to all those who believe that bipartisan compromise is always the best course. She believed that moderates in her own party were partially responsible for prolonging Britain's socialist oriented policies because they lacked "moral courage" and "time and again … [were] prepared to compromise their positions."[47]

Thatcher succeeded in bringing Britain back from the abyss by reining in the Labour Party's special interest allies - trade unions; by reducing government borrowing; by privatizing state-controlled industry; and by reducing the burden on the private sector through lower taxes and fewer regulatory controls. In fact, as biographer Moore highlights she reduced Britain's crushing tax burden from a "top rate of 98% in 1979 to 40% in 1988."[48] By the time she left office in 1990, Thatcher's memoirs make clear that the British economy was off life support and growing. Instead of borrowing 9 % of GDP a year, they repaid some debt, public spending-to-GDP fell, inflation dropped significantly, the annual GDP growth rate doubled and the "number of people in jobs rose by 1.5 million in the 1980s."[49]

After 11 years of successful free enterprise government in Great Britain she exposed, once again before she left office, the fallacies of the socialist inspired arguments that are critical of the top percentage of income earners. In a forceful exchange in the House of Commons captured on You Tube she responded to a question by a member of the opposition. (A visit to www.Youtube .com/watch?v=okHGCz6xxiw to see the Iron Lady in action is recommended.) She tells Parliament that when the opposition complains about the "gap" between the top 10% of wage earners and the bottom 10% what they are really saying is that - so long as the gap is smaller under their socialist- inspired policies - they would rather see "the bottom 10% poorer "just as long as they can make the top 10% "less rich." To the cheers of many in Parliament, she says she "hit the nail on the head" and concludes that by making wealth gaps smaller with the "poor becoming poorer" and the rich "less rich" that you will never "create wealth and opportunity" and improve the lives of all. For all those who have considered putting their faith in Obama's class warfare strategy of attacking the so-called wealthy as the panacea for our nation's ills, the Iron Lady tells us that ploy has been tried before and failed.[50]

Based on Britain's near economic collapse after 30 years of regulatory overreach and wealth redistributionist policies, it seems clear that all those who are concerned about generational theft as a result of the Obama administration policies have a legitimate point that cries out for a cure. As The Iron Lady's experience teaches, there is hope that with a government that is "limited" in scope and supportive of the private sector and the "rule of law," our great economy can also spring back to life.

CHAPTER 9

Obama "Ratchets Up" ILL-Gotten Gains

America has been successful over the centuries because of a "common core of agreed-upon beliefs." These beliefs depend on the Rule of Law for "broad legal limits" and occasional "patching up" but not for laws that cripple the American spirit and dynamic individualism. One leading 20th century historian succinctly captured these ideas for us. As we have seen, these are basically the same principles that Thatcher and Reagan made the cornerstone of their successful governing philosophies. As Richard Hofstadter tells us in *The American Political Tradition*:

"The sanctity of private property, the right of the individual to dispose of and invest it, the value of opportunity, and the natural evolution of self interest and self assertion, within broad legal limits ... have been staple tenets of the central faith in American political ideologies ....The business of politics ... is to protect this competitive world, to foster it on occasion, to patch up its incidental abuses, but not to cripple it with a plan for collective action .... Almost the entire span of American history under the present Constitution has coincided with the rise and spread of modern industrial capitalism. In material power and productivity, the United States has been a flourishing success. Societies that are in such good working order have a kind of mute organic consistency. *They do not foster ideas that are hostile to their fundamental working arrangements.*" (Emphasis supplied)[1]

In his first term in office, Obama has recorded "the four highest deficits since 1946 ... increasing the federal debt by about $5 trillion in a mere four years."[2] In this connection, Obama has shown an unprecedented capacity for supporting wealth redistributionist legislation and regulatory intervention that blatantly ignore these "core ... beliefs." The signature laws of his first term - the American Recovery and Reinvestment Act of 2009 (Stimulus Act), the 2010 Patient Protection and Affordable Care Act (Obama Care) and the Wall Street Reform and Consumer Protection Act (Dodd-Frank) and the regulations they have spawned, are prime examples of laws that meet the so-called "legality" test. But they clearly violate one or more of the rule of law principles. And empirical data also tell us such lawmaking squelches economic growth.

There is little doubt as MIT researchers have found based on a "broad panel of countries over thirty years ..." that "with respect to government policies ... better maintenance of the rule of law" and less "government spending - and the associated taxation" are key "determinants of economic growth."[3] The Heritage Foundation's most recent analysis of economic policy developments in 184 countries, its *2012 Index of Economic Freedom*, confirms the MIT research. Like MIT's data, the "rule of law" and "limited government" are key positive components in its analysis of economic freedom and the growth and prosperity that results from economic freedom. On the other hand, The Heritage Foundation found that "rapid expansion of government, more than any market factor, appears to be responsible for flagging economic dynamism. Government spending has not only failed to arrest the economic crisis, but also - in many countries - seems to prolong it."[4] Edward Fuelner, President of The Heritage Foundation, tells us how the U.S. performed in the index. "How about the U.S., historically the country more responsible than any other for leading the march of freedom? Under President Barack Obama, it has moved to the back of the band. It has dropped to 10th place overall .... Government expenditures have grown to a level equivalent to over 40% of GDP, and total public debt exceeds the size of the economy."[5]

And "the little guys," who can't afford lobbyists to take advantage of the loopholes in the government's rule of law charade, lose disproportionately when government programs overwhelm business and personal economic freedoms. To prove a point, as of March 2012, the unemployment rate for Hispanics was 10.7% and for blacks 14.1%. "The black unemployment rate is now twice the rate for whites, and those without a college degree are still more than twice as likely to be unemployed than those with a diploma."[6]

As Professor Todd Zywicki of George Mason University Law School tells us, "[f]rom the myriad special interest provisions marbleized throughout Dodd-Frank, to the arbitrary process of granting waivers from the mandates of Obama care to favored applicants, to the pork-laden "green" subsidies [think Solyndra solar panel scandal and the taxpayers $500,000,000.00 loss] and "stimulus" bill enacted soon after President Obama took office, the … relationship between government discretion and special interest rent seeking [looking for politicians to dole out political favors] has been on full display in the post crisis period. Huge swaths of the economy - health care, banking, energy, auto manufacturing and probably others - have become utterly politicized as economic success has come to be defined by one's ability to buy and sell political favors rather than one's ability to meet consumer demand efficiently. When economic success results from one's relative ability to operate the levers of power, the ultimate winners are big business and big labor. Goldman Sachs, General Motors, the SEIU, and the UAW can hire the lawyers and lobbyists to create and exploit loopholes in the legal system to advance their narrow interests at the expense of the public at large. *Conversely, the prime beneficiaries of constraining government behavior by the rule of law are the little guys who lack the time, money, or interest required to manipulate the levers of government discretion to their advantage."* (Emphasis supplied).[7] Consequently, as Zywicki concludes "[t]he lesson of past economic crises as well as the most recent crisis … is that we should uphold the rule of law with special rigor in times of economic crisis because the temptations for politicians to misuse their powers during times of crisis are especially great."[8]

But instead of upholding the Rule of Law, Obama - as he learned from radical professor Unger - used the recent economic crisis as the once- in- a- life- time opportunity to wreak havoc on the Rule of Law and move the U.S. even further away from its roots. The federal government seized "broad discretionary control" under Roosevelt's New Deal agenda. It laid the "foundation for the rise of the administrative state" and is the classic "historical example" of the "ratchet effect" that is largely responsible for suffocating economic growth today.[9] So, not to let any lingering effects of the crisis go unused as he gets ready for a hoped for second-term, Obama has "ratcheted up" the rule of law violations of his first four years in office.

Obama continues his class warfare agenda by proposing that the so-called Buffett tax rule should apply to all those making more than $1 million a year so that, in Obama's words, they pay their "fair share."

This class of people will get the privilege of paying a *minimum* 30% tax rate while about half of Americans pay no federal income tax at all.[10] Looking at recent data The Heritage Foundation indicates, "[t]hat means 151.7 million Americans paid nothing in 2009. By comparison, 34.8 million tax filers paid no taxes in 1984."[11] Obama would also increase taxes on all households making more than $250,000 and raise the top rate this class of people pay on "dividends" to the same 39.6%, so that they also pay their "fair share."[12]

Never mind that the top 3%, or those making more than $200,000.00 for individuals and $250,000 for couples per year currently pay more in income taxes than the remaining 97%. And I suppose we should also not be concerned that the new proposed dividend rate - when combined with other proposed tax increases and the phase out of deductions and exemptions - will nearly triple the dividend rate from the current 15%. Ultimately this class warfare proposal hurts all shareholders, especially retirees, as companies cut back on paying dividends and stock prices drop.[13] And don't think that the middle class will escape the Obama tax man's grasp now that the Supreme Court has deemed the "penalty" for violating the individual mandate in Obama Care to be a "tax." As Senate Minority Leader, Mitch McConnell, tells us "The president said it was not a tax, and the Supreme Court, which has the final say, said it is a tax, [t]he tax is going to be levied, 77 percent of it will be levied on Americans making less than $120,000 a year. So it's a middle-class tax increase."[14]

Bernie Madoff would have been proud of the Obama administration and its congressional Democratic allies since it got away with a massive cover-up of the root cause of our current financial crisis. The Dodd-Frank financial reform legislation punished the financial industry alone for the root cause of the crisis - decades of misguided government mortgage lending policies - and white-washed the roles of the leading culprits, Senator Dodd and Congressman Frank. Then seizing another opportunity to obfuscate the root cause of the crisis the Obama administration, along with politically ambitious state attorneys general, "ratcheted up" the Dodd-Frank ill- gotten gains and negotiated a $25 billion settlement with five leading banks because of mortgage foreclosure paper processing irregularities involving so-called "robo-signers." While most of the media appear to have gullibly followed the government's talking points when reporting on this settlement, it had nothing to do with the original housing bubble crisis.

University of Pennsylvania Law School Professor, David Skeel, is not confused by the atmospherics surrounding the settlement. He concludes that the "biggest loser is the rule of law" in this "mortgage shakedown" of Bank of America, Citigroup, J.P. Morgan Chase, Wells Fargo, and Ally Financial. He goes on to point out, "without the full protections afforded by a lawsuit, the government in effect extorted billions from the banks to provide another stimulus to housing without going to congress ….Throughout the financial crisis, starting with the bailouts of Bear Stearns and AIG, and continuing with the auto bailouts, the government has assumed that normal rules and restrictions, not to mention constitutional checks and balances don't matter. So far it has prevailed, but at considerable cost. By cutting corners to achieve desired ends, government intervention has created clouds of uncertainty that will linger long after the crisis has passed."[15]

Not learning the lessons taught us from years of failed fuel economy standards, Obama has also proposed that auto manufacturers double the fuel economy of their fleets by 2025. This would increase the fleet average standard called CAFÉ from the original 27.5 maximum to 54.5 miles per gallon, apparently based on the agreement of the auto industry itself.[16] Taking into consideration that the General Motors and Chrysler of the second decade of the 21st century have little room to object to the government's new extreme fuel economy demands because the bailouts put them under the thumb of the federal government, the CAFÉ standards, among other things, have always played fast and loose with rule of law principles because they mock the requirement of "certainty." Surprisingly as it may sound, compliance with the standards for which millions of dollars of fines can be imposed, if they are not met, is ultimately out of the manufacturers' hands. This bizarre situation arises because compliance depends upon the vehicles that consumers choose to buy each model year so the manufacturer does not know with "certainty" at the beginning of the model year whether it will or will not meet the standards. If consumers purchase too many of a manufacturers less fuel efficient but more popular vehicles, the manufacturer can be fined at the end of the year. To avoid the fines, if possible, the manufacturer - sometime during the model- year run - will have to scramble and push more smaller, lighter weight fuel efficient vehicles on fleets and consumers at deep discounts to offset the larger vehicles that consumers really want to buy. This is akin to the federal government setting standards that result in Apple Inc. being fined if consumers purchase more iPads than iPhones. Can you believe that Silicon Valley and their customers would stand for such domination over their products?

So after GM exited from bankruptcy in 2009, after decades of struggling to meet revenue-draining and inefficient federal fuel economy standards (on top of the costs of questionable emissions standards considering most of the air pollution problem came from older, poorly maintained cars and never-ending union demands), the Obama administration is doubling down.[17] This rule of law travesty hits close to home inasmuch as I was the first staff lawyer on the GM legal staff in Detroit to be responsible for providing advice to GM employees relative to the fuel economy standards, which became effective in the mid-1970s. There is little question that under the government's recent fuel economy mandates, consumer choice will get trampled upon even more so than in the past as government controls replace the natural influence of "prices" to determine what products consumers will or will not purchase. And there is little doubt that consumers will suffer motor vehicle safety tradeoffs under the government's dictates.

It appears that the Obama administration's underlying motive is to trade off higher new car prices and crash safety for fuel economy increasing technology and vehicle design changes to placate the environmental lobby's preoccupation with so-called global climate change. Consumers clearly come out on the short end of this stick on this deal. They can ill afford to pay for these higher priced, smaller vehicles especially in our sputtering economy. And there is little question that more car crash fatalities will result when these smaller lighter weight vehicles impact larger vehicles -such as the SUVs that the President runs around in. Higher fuel economy standards supposedly will reduce the so-called "carbon footprint." In exchange, thousands of car accident victims and economic pain will be sacrificed on the environmental altar for questionable "global warming" concerns 50 to 100 years from now. As the prestigious *Car and Driver* magazine said when Obama took his first crack at mandating higher fuel economy standards in 2009, what we end up with under stringent fuel economy standards are "expensive, tiny cars" that are not the choice of the car buying public.[18]

Ultimately, the price of gasoline and not federal regulation is the most important reason for consumers purchasing more fuel-efficient vehicles and the number of miles a person drives. And if the government is really interested in reducing dependence on imported sources of oil, which is the purported reason for the extreme standards, "the best way to do so is to eliminate the extensive federal restrictions on domestic oil exploration and development."[19]

Not only did decades of misguided federal standards result in thousands of lost jobs, they also resulted in a wasteful drain on the companies' revenue, loss of consumer choice and thousands of deaths and injuries that resulted from the smaller lighter weight cars that manufacturers were forced to sell to meet the standards. One study found that just between the beginning of the mandated fuel economy standards in 1975 and 1998 that "46,000 people have died in crashes that they would have survived if they had been traveling in bigger, heavier cars."[20] In the late 1970s and early 1980s, as a response to the regulatory abuse and overreach from the Carter administration, I served as the Attorney-in-charge of Regulatory Litigation on the GM legal staff. In that assignment, we tried to keep the government honest and protect our rule of law rights by litigating with the EPA and challenging its regulatory abuses in connection with emissions and fuel economy issues. (I left GM in 1991 to join a law firm in Washington, D.C.) It appears that in 2012, the Obama administration has given the auto industry an "attitude adjustment" and the will to stand up to the federal government - with "Big Brother" Obama at the controls - is not what it used to be.

The Catholic Church, in particular, and religious freedom, in general, have also become casualties of the Obama administration's "ratcheting up" the rule of law defeat in connection with the passage of Obama Care. After assuming control of virtually all personal health care decisions in the Obama Care legislation, the Obama administration's Department of Health and Human Services decided in August 2011 that it could run roughshod over the Catholic Church's religious beliefs and the constitutional protections of the First Amendment in connection with contraception. Disregarding the Catholic Church's doctrine on contraception it ordered all Catholic hospitals and other institutions that insure their employees to cover various forms of contraception. While Obama partially backtracked on his agency's order in February 2012 - more in the form of political maneuvering than substantive revisions to preserve religious freedom - this was just one more example of the administration's assault on the Rule of Law.[21]

By May 2012, the University of Notre Dame and other Catholic organizations had had enough of fruitless discussions with the Obama administration to find a principled compromise and filed lawsuits in federal courts around the country to protect their religious freedoms from the unprecedented mandate of the federal government. Pertinent excerpts from the May 21, 2012 letter of Father John Jenkins, President of the University of Notre Dame, to the Notre Dame community leave no doubt about the importance of the university's stand on this issue to all Americans who cherish the constitution and religious freedom. "Today the University of Notre Dame filed a lawsuit ... regarding a recent mandate from the U.S. Department of Health and Human Services .... The mandate requires Notre Dame and similar religious organizations to provide in their insurance plans abortion-inducing drugs, contraceptives and sterilization procedures, which are contrary to catholic teaching .... This filing is about the freedom of a religious organization to live its mission, and its significance goes well beyond any debate about contraceptives. For if we concede that the Government can decide which religious organizations are sufficiently religious to be awarded the freedom to follow the principles that define their mission, then we have begun to walk down a path that ultimately leads to the undermining of those institutions. For if one Presidential Administration can override our religious purpose and use religious organizations to advance policies that undercut our values, then surely another Administration will do the same for a very different set of policies, each time invoking some concept of popular will or the public good, with the result these religious organizations become mere tools for the exercise of government power, morally subservient to the state, and not free from its infringements. If that happens, it will be the end of genuinely religious organizations in all but name."[22]

And regardless of your religious beliefs, don't think that allowing the bureaucrats to make decisions that are not based on the Rule of Law has little impact on your daily lives. It is literally a matter of life and death. The FDA's denial of its earlier approval for the world's leading cancer drug should make all those who have or will have breast cancer in the future take notice. In what has been called "a chillingly blunt assertion of regulatory power" in a November 18, 2011 decision by the Commissioner of the Food and Drug Administration, Margaret Hamburg, the FDA withdrew approval for the life saving drug, Avastin. Her decision claimed that approval requires "credible, objective evidence." But the agency offers no definition of what the "credible or objective evidence" might be that would support approval. This kind of naked assertion of power is exactly what the rule of law ideal has historically prevented.[23]

But if you think that the FDA has overstepped the bounds of the Rule of Law, a key bureaucrat at Obama's EPA unveils for all of us what may lie ahead in a second- term Obama presidency as Obama's acolytes take off the gloves to punish the American free enterprise system and undermine our legal protections. As part of an investigation of the EPA by Oklahoma Republican Senator James Inhofe, the senator discovered a videotape of a 2010 lecture given by one of the EPA's regional leaders for Oklahoma, Texas and other states in the area. In the videotape released by the senator in April 2012, the EPA official let his guard down and confided to his audience what the EPA really thinks about due process and other rule of law niceties when it comes to EPA's view of how the government should treat oil and gas companies. Putting aside the fact that companies that produce oil and gas provide the energy that sustains our very lives by powering everything from our hospitals to our military's defense machinery, the EPA official explained to his audience that their "'philosophy of enforcement' is 'like how the Romans used to conquer little villages in the Mediterranean. They'd go into a little Turkish town somewhere, they'd find the first five guys they saw and they would crucify them. And you know the town was really easy to manage for the next few years.'"[24]

The rule of law ideal necessitates that government officials make decisions impartially based on fixed and predictable rules and procedures. Otherwise we descend into a "government of men or women" over a "government of laws" - precisely what happened here when government officials start to believe that they have the right to trample on the legal rights of American businesses, and the men and women who depend on those businesses for their livelihood, or in EPA's words to "crucify them." Beyond the few examples given above, Obama's administration has brought new meaning to regulatory overreach as the EPA, FDA, DOE, ICE, Department of Homeland Security, Interior

Department, the Department of Health and Human Services and the Consumer Financial Protection Bureau, to name a few, are suffocating business and stagnating consumer demand in the U.S. The number of new major regulations issued just during Obama's first 26 months is staggering and the costs to society is unparalleled in our history. The Heritage Foundation provides some sobering facts: "During its first 26 months - from taking office to mid-FY 2011 --the Obama administration has imposed 75 new major regulations .... The annual cost of regulation—$1.75 trillion by one frequently cited estimate - represents twice the amount of individual income taxes collected last year. Overall, from the beginning of the Obama administration to mid-fiscal year (FY) 2011, regulators have imposed $38 billion in new costs on the American people, more than any comparable period on record. Consider Washington's red tape to be a hidden tax."[25]

Commenting on the regulatory crisis in 2012 America - which could overwhelm America in Obama's second term as he takes his "ratcheting up" strategy to new heights - the prestigious *Economist* magazine warns that America "is being suffocated by excessive and badly written regulations." It highlights as support a Small Business Administration study that has found that regulations in America add "$10,585 per employee" and that given such an extraordinary burden on American business, the magazine points out "it's a wonder the jobless rate isn't even higher than it is." The *Economist* goes on to emphasize that "Democrats write rules to expand the welfare state." And using the Dodd-Frank banking regulation law as an example, the magazine tells us that while it may have had a "noble" purpose, it is "843 pages" long and almost "every other page demands that regulators fill in further detail .... When a bill is hundreds of pages long," *The Economist* points out, "it is not hard for congressmen to slip in clauses that benefit their chums and campaign donors [and that, in particular,] the health-care bill included tons of favors for the pushy." It goes on to highlight that of the "400 rules it [Dodd-Frank] mandates, only 93 have been finalized. So financial firms in America must prepare to comply with a law that is partly unintelligible and partly unknowable."

In identifying problems with Obama's health-care law, which should be of even more concern now that the Supreme Court failed to strike down the individual mandate, the *Economist* opens our eyes to the fact that in 2013 Obama Care will significantly increase the burdens of an already complex system. "Next year the number of federally mandated categories of illness and injury for which hospitals may claim reimbursement will rise from 18,000 to 140,000. *There are nine codes relating to injuries caused by parrots, and three relating to burns from flaming water skis.*" (Emphasis supplied.) And it does not appear to the *Economist* that the Obama administration is serious about fixing the problem. It points out that "Democrats pay lip service to the need to slim the rulebook ..." and that when it comes to their putative justification for the rules, the "[Obama] administration has a bias towards overstating the benefits and understating the costs." The respected publication concludes that unless America's lawmakers rein in "[o]ver-regulated America ... by making regulators "more accountable" and the rules "much simpler" and less "complex"... America has a "real danger: that regulation may crush the life out of America's economy."[26]

Thus, contrary to the rule of law principles of "generality," "equality" of application and "certainty," Obama's legislative and regulatory initiatives have "ratcheted up" the welfare state legacy first put in place by FDR and left American society bitterly divided along class lines, uncertain and stagnated. For the factory worker unemployment is at near record highs and the businessman or investor does not know when the next regulatory roadblock or tax increase shoe will drop and all homeowners have lost so much equity in their homes that they have to reach up to touch bottom.

CHAPTER 10

OBAMA'S SECOND TERM: THE TIPPING POINT

What the *Economist*, other media and the public do not realize is that Obama's preoccupation with "bureaucratic or regulatory law" has a much deeper importance to someone schooled in his Harvard Professor Unger's radical philosophy. In Unger's way of thinking - which Obama has clearly adopted-- "bureaucratic law becomes a tool of the power interests of the group that controls the state" and without question, as Unger admits, violates the Rule of Law. Unger was quite clear in his treatise on how the Rule of Law has or can be undermined by "bureaucratic law." He points out that "the commands of the sovereign (in this case Obama and his allies) in systems of bureaucratic law often take the form of rules applicable to general categories of persons and acts. But this will be a generality of political expedience ... that may and will be violated whenever the considerations of administrative efficiency that led to its adoption point the other way."

In short, Unger showed that historically bureaucratic law is related to the "prince's command and subject to his almost unlimited discretion." And that the lack of favoritism or, in other words, the "generality" sought by the Rule of Law will be trotted out only as a "matter of expedience" in a society that is dominated by "bureaucratic law."[1] There is little question that Obama learned his "bureaucratic law" lessons well as his administration has issued one "prince[ly] command" after another in which agency after agency has sought to exercise virtually "unlimited discretion." And if you think this is an exaggeration, recall the EPA official we learned about in the last chapter who confided that EPA's philosophy is to "crucify" in enforcement proceedings selected oil and gas companies to coerce other companies into obeying EPA's commands.

The anecdotal evidence of President Obama's take on the Rule of Law is also alarming and just one more piece of evidence alongside his legislative and regulatory record over the last four years. When Wisconsin state legislators were hiding out in neighboring Illinois in early 2011 - so that they would not have to vote on a deficit-reducing measure to rein in public employee unions - instead of criticizing this rule of law travesty he, in fact, supported their recklessness.[2] When an African-American Harvard professor was confronted by a white police officer in Cambridge, MA in the summer of 2009, Obama insulted the Cambridge police by claiming they acted "stupidly" before all of the facts were available, thus denying them basic "due process" rights. Obama had to back pedal from his intemperate comments once the facts came in.[3]

When criticizing Arizona's immigration law in the spring of 2010 he misled the American public by claiming that an illegal immigrant could be picked up by the police and harassed for immigration law violations if you simply "took your kid out to get ice cream." Copying the tricks of slick trial lawyers, in his half-truth he failed to mention the critical precondition in the Arizona law - that one's immigration status could only be checked if the person was otherwise stopped for an unrelated violation of law.[4] The Supreme Court clearly did not buy this kind of misleading racial profiling argument. In its June 25, 2012 decision, the Court upheld the so-called "stop and check" provision in the Arizona law, SB 1070. In ruling in favor of Arizona on the stop and check provision, the Court recognized that SB 1070 only authorized state law enforcement officials to check a person's immigration status when "they stop, detain or arrest a person on some other legitimate basis."[5] It had to be clear to Obama - just like it was to the Supreme Court - that SB 1070 only authorized the police to check a person's immigration status if the individual had been arrested or detained for another offense. We can thus conclude our president intentionally left out of his "ice cream" scenario that the father would have had to have been caught trying to rob the ice cream shop before his immigration status could be checked.

And when the Obama administration tired of being hassled by the requirements imposed by immigration law and the failure of Congress to pass legislation that would give amnesty to illegal aliens in college, under the proposed Dream Act, it just ordered its administrative agency to handle the problem without congressional approval.

Obama's Second Term: The Tipping Point

In a June 2011 memo from the Enforcement Director of the Obama administration's Immigration and Customs Enforcement agency, ICE, the Enforcement Director - for all intents and purposes - told ICE agents not to enforce deportation laws for thousands of illegal aliens already in the legal system if, among other factors, they were not "serious felons" with criminal records.[6] And a year later as the 2012 election approached, Obama decided to take his mockery of the Rule of Law one step further. In June 2012, by executive order he directed the Department of Homeland Security to simply stop deporting upwards of a million illegal aliens under the age of 30, who were brought to the U.S. as children, if they meet certain minimal conditions that are similar to those in the proposed DREAM Act that Congress did not pass![7] In light of Obama's disregard for constitutionally mandated law-making steps, it's probably time to conclude that Obama now believes he is the "Prince" that Unger talked about in his book who manipulates regulatory law to suit his own personal agenda.

Some of this disregard for the Rule of Law could possibly be excused if we were not dealing with a president who has a long-standing disrespect for American legal principles as evidenced by his own observations captured in his memoirs. And surely he stands apart from his recent predecessors in the Oval Office in that he was mentored by a hardcore liberal constitutional law professor, Laurence Tribe, who was the key figure in torpedoing Ronald Reagan's 1986 Supreme Court nomination of a bona fide rule of law oriented judge -Robert Bork. And to go one better, he was indoctrinated at the Harvard Law School in courses such as "Reinventing Democracy" by a self-proclaimed revolutionary professor. And recall what went on in this small, intense course. One of Obama's classmates observed that in Professor Unger's class they "first inspected and then undermined the presumptions of American legal thought."[8]

There is no question that Obama understands the legal principles that needed to be undermined. While described a little differently in his *Audacity of Hope* memoir, he explicitly recognizes the basic attributes of the Rule of Law which he acknowledged were accepted by political theorists even before the American Revolution: "laws constraining liberty [should be] uniform, predictable, transparent, and apply equally to rulers and ruled."[9] He also stressed in his book the importance of adhering to "established senate voting procedures" because "arguments over Senate procedures do matter ….." As he correctly pointed out - but later failed to follow - "the procedural rules of our government help define results …. They define our democracy just as much as expectations do."[10]

Incredible as it may seem in light of his administration's immigration enforcement record, he also emphasized in his memoirs the importance of adhering to rule of law principles in connection with immigration enforcement. In 2006, when meeting with an immigrant advocacy group that was protesting certain deportations, he told them "American citizenship is a privilege and not a right … [and] that without meaningful borders and respect for the law … opportunities and protections afforded those who live in this country would surely erode."[11]

It is said that one has to know the opposition before you can develop a counter strategy. In this regard, he sure succeeded. As we have seen, Obama was taught to first understand the traditional legal principles and then to "undermine" them. The passage of Obama Care and the administration's immigration law enforcement end-runs during his first term are stand-out examples. In fact, the Obama administration's failure to enforce immigration laws is so blatant that during the April 2012 arguments before the Supreme Court over the federal government's lawsuit against Arizona's immigration law, Chief Justice Roberts commented that it "seems to me the federal government doesn't want to know who's here illegally or not."[12]

And Obama Care was passed in 2010 after the Democrats engaged in a public display of horse-trading among senators to give them billions for their respective states to get their votes - activities that looked a lot like bribery to the public - even if they didn't get their booty in the final bill. Then, as we have seen earlier, they had to ditch the long-established senate voting procedure in early 2010 - which requires 60 votes in the senate to avoid a filibuster - to pass the amended, or in reality, the final bill after Senator Ted Kennedy passed away. Instead, Obama and his allies - Harry Reid in the senate - with help from speaker of the House Nancy Pelosi – played fast and loose with the Senate voting procedures. They used an arcane parliamentary budget procedure called reconciliation- occasionally used for tax and spending legislation - to scrape up at least a of 51 votes. This was short of the 60 votes needed under the long- established senate voting procedures. But enough votes to pass the final amended version of Obama Care, while denying the opposition

Republicans an opportunity to exercise their filibuster rights that could have resulted in a compromise bill the American public would have found acceptable. Senate Minority Leader, Mitch Mc Connell, did not let the Democrats' manipulation go unchallenged. In February, 2010 he decried their effort as "arrogant" and nothing more than an attempt to "use whatever device is available to jam down the throats" of the American public a bill they did not want. He made it perfectly clear that in the history of the Senate reconciliation had "never been used for this kind of systemic [massive government takeover of health care] reform."[13]

The bottom line is that Obama's respect for "established senate voting procedures" - that he trumpeted in his *Audacity of Hope* memoir - when it looked like Republicans would use a majority only voting procedure or so-called "nuclear option" to avoid a Democrat party filibuster a few years earlier when he was a Senator - was short lived. When these pesky procedures got in the way of his personal rule of law end run he quickly threw them under the bus. And when it was convenient in his 2006 memoir to extol the virtues of respecting our borders and meeting immigration law's requirements, once in office non-enforcement and amnesty offered through ICE became the strategies of the day.

Sadly, the adulteration of the Rule of Law does not stop at the courthouse steps. I led Suzuki's national efforts to fight an onslaught of frivolous lawsuits involving the Suzuki Samurai sport utility vehicle in the 1990s and early 2000s and was lead counsel in Suzuki's multi-year lawsuit against *Consumer Reports* magazine for product disparagement. In these assignments, I saw firsthand the carnage that results to a company - usually at the urging of avaricious trial attorneys - when judges abuse their discretion and play fast and loose with the Rule of Law. My national litigation background provided unforgettable lessons: when judges such as those President Obama favors are inclined to meet "social consequences" or "empathetic" ends in their decision-making, it is clear to me that such platitudes are simply code for achieving a personal agenda that tramples all over the rule of law rights of all concerned with supposed deep pockets, whether auto manufacturers, doctors or small business owners.[14] And as consumers we all pay in the end.

Beyond Obama's rule of law avoidance in the legislative and regulatory arenas, he has not been asleep on the job as it relates to the judiciary. The Roosevelt intimidation game plan has already been initiated by Barack Obama. He publicly ridiculed the Supreme Court justices during his 2010 State of the Union address for their decision to strike down parts of a federal statute under the First Amendment. In the *Citizens United* case, the Supreme Court ruled that the statute was unconstitutional because it denied corporations their First Amendment right to contribute to independent causes during an election and thereby to participate fully in federal elections, much to the chagrin of the corporation-bashing Democrats.

And, as we have seen from an earlier chapter, in early April 2012, shortly after the Supreme Court's oral arguments in the Obama Care case he went on the attack again. In public comments, he not only insulted the Supreme Court by referring to them "as unelected people" but took the more reckless and erroneous step of warning the Supreme Court that overturning Obama Care "would be an unprecedented, extraordinary step [since] the law "was passed by a strong majority of a democratically elected Congress." We must first take note of his "strong majority" misrepresentation inasmuch as Obama's acolytes Reid and Pelosi had to bypass the long- established senate voting procedures - which required 60 votes to avoid a filibuster - to cobble up enough votes to pass the amended or final bill. But more to the point relative to Obama's "unprecedented "claim, based on over 200 years of precedent - remember the *Marbury* case of 1803 highlighted earlier - it is the Supreme Court's duty to overturn laws that exceed constitutional bounds regardless of how many votes they received in congress. In fact, just between the years of 1953 and 1997, the Supreme Court struck down, 74 separate statutory provisions in acts of Congress, so the only thing "unprecedented" about the court overturning Obama Care is that it would have slowed down Obama's march to gut the rule of law and make the U.S. a "government of men" as opposed to a "government of laws."[15] Unfortunately, Chief Justice Roberts and the liberal faction on the Supreme Court, who joined him in upholding the individual mandate in the June, 2012 Obama Care decision, must not be overly troubled with a "government of men" over a "government of laws."

As we learned in an earlier chapter, his mentor at the Harvard Law School - the left leaning Harvard Professor Tribe - took long walks with law student Obama instead of requiring him to do basic legal research. Based on his intimidation effort, it looks as though Obama might have benefitted from less time strolling with Tribe and a little more research time in the library where he might have discovered the *Marbury* case. And we have seen from previous chapters that Roosevelt tried to pack the court with additional justices favorable to his New Deal legislation by expanding the court to 15 justices from nine almost immediately after he won his second term victory in 1936. (It should be kept in mind that the economy in the 1930s picked up somewhat before Roosevelt's 1936 victory and then descended again in 1937 so voters should not be lulled into complaisance if the 2012 economy picks up before the 2012 election.) All Obama has to do is to gain the White House again in 2012 and wait for one of the current conservative majority on the court to pass away or retire. A second term may very well give him that opportunity inasmuch as justices Scalia and Kennedy are currently over 70 years of age. His opportunity to stack the court with younger, left-leaning justices who are more "empathetic" instead of rule of law grounded and share Tribe's views of the left's "mushy" self-serving view of the rule of law, has already begun with the appointments of justices Sotomayor and Kagan to the court in his first term.

If liberal justices Ginsburg and Breyer - who are also over 70, retire or pass away while Obama is in office, he may be able to put his ideological stamp on the Supreme Court with as many as four or more justices. In a second term - if he can appoint an ideologically like-minded majority to the Supreme Court - Obama and his unelected agency bureaucrats may enjoy the long-term benefits of a favorable Supreme Court behind them. Then they will be in a better position – especially with the help of the new Obama Care taxing power prec-edent – to tax the public into submission. Without serious Supreme Court opposition, the federal government could tell you what car to drive, pills to take, what to eat, where you can use your credit card and - stepping into God's shoes - when to die.

The importance to our Republic of a Supreme Court bench with justices who respect the traditional understanding of the Rule of Law cannot be overemphasized. The contrast between rule of law oriented judges - as opposed to those who want to achieve their personal view of preferable "social consequences" through a "living" Constitution for instance - could not be clearer. As we have seen, Hayek drew a bright line distinction between this freewheeling approach to decision-mak-ing by judges and their historically validated role based on the Rule of Law. As he explained "[i]t is because the judge who applies them [rules] has no choice in drawing the conclusions that follow from the existing body of rules and the particular facts of the case that it can be said that laws and not men govern."[16]

Supreme Court chief Justice, John Marshall, a man responsible for some of this country's most important constitutional law principles and Justice Scalia on the current court echo Hayek's profound observations. Recall that Chief Justice Marshall, one of this country's earliest and most-respected Chief Justices, early in the nineteenth century clearly defined the limited decision-making role of a judge when he intoned, "Courts are mere instruments of law, and can will nothing."[17] (It appears from the Obama Care decision that Chief Justice Roberts disagrees with the great Chief Justice, John Marshall, and believes his "will" and not the "law" is supreme.)

The reader will recall that Justice Scalia's view - nearly two hundred years after Marshall's - is perfectly consistent: "The rule of law is about form …. Long live formalism. It is what makes a government of laws and not men…. By trying to make the constitution to do everything that needs doing from age to age [by judicial interpretation], we shall have caused it to do nothing at all."[18]

With a Supreme Court that tosses aside the "blind justice" demanded by the rule of law ideal, Obama would have the Supreme Court as a backup to uphold or strike down laws or cases that were ideologically inconsistent with a left-leaning worldview regardless of what congress or the American public believe is right for our country.[19] And let's remember, changes on the Supreme Court should not be viewed as a short-term problem as its ideological reach could last long after Obama leaves office, if he wins a second term.

While the talking heads in the media cannot get enough of the political story or scandal of the day, if you are concerned about yourself in retirement down the road or what effect the laws will have on your children or grandchildren, you should never forget some reality oriented observations from Professor Tamanaha of St John's University School of Law: "Political coalitions for legislation come and go, but achieving a critical mass of like-minded judges can lock in the dominance of a set of ideological views for a generation. Furthermore, judges can trump or constrain the political process through judicial review or by eviscerating statutes and regulations with narrow interpretations."[20]

Just as Roosevelt's effort to ditch long-standing legal principles to accomplish his ideological goals resulted in economic failure, so has Barack Obama's. The importance of "certainty" in laws as emphasized by history's great thinkers - starting with Cicero - and the resulting ability it gives everyone to manage their business and personal lives are paramount in a free society. The ability to predict when, where, and how much government will intrude into our lives are hallmarks of liberty and the Rule of Law. Taking over the reins of government in a period of economic stress, Obama's efforts to destroy the Rule of Law with wealth redistributionist legislation, a flurry of ideologically motivated regulations, appointments of like-minded judges - with the probability of more Supreme Court appointments to come - and his public displays of rule of law bashing have resulted in the current legal and economic crises. With the Obama administration's rule of law "uncertainty" score topping the charts, we are left with staggering debt, many millions unemployed and investors confused about America's economic future.

Before Obama was ever elected in 2008, the Rule of Law was on life support. Its weakened condition was due largely to FDR's sweeping agenda that virtually ignored rule of law principles, the legal skepticism that swept over the U.S. during the anti-establishment Vietnam era, and to the rule of law's careless disregard by politicians on either side of the aisle over the last few decades.

Add to this status quo Obama's background, his inveterate biases about traditional American legal principles and business and his first-term efforts to undermine the Rule of Law, we will have reached the "tipping point." There seems to be little doubt that President Obama's prejudices and radical political "theology," as one former presidential candidate called it, has impelled him to attempt to destroy America's rule of law foundation or, in other words, the DNA that has allowed this country to be a "government of laws and not men" from our birth in the 18th century.

The record shows that Obama knew full well what the rule of law principles were long before he became president and that his policies and actions nevertheless thwarted this ideal at just about every turn, resulting in a needlessly prolonged recession. As the respected former Senator from Texas, Phil Gramm, and a former congressional budget expert recently told the public, "[n]ever before in postwar

America …" has the recovery been so slow and "painful"… resulting in "record high poverty levels, record low teenage employment, record high long term unemployment, shrinking birthrates, exploding welfare benefits, and a crippled middle class." They go on to point out what the American public could have expected if Obama had followed the successful economic policies of Ronald Reagan instead of the failed policies of Franklin Roosevelt. If Obama had not implemented the "equally absurd" policies that Franklin Roosevelt tried decades before involving "unprecedented spending," "equally destructive tax policy" and "tirades" against the so-called rich, "[s]ome 16.9 million more Americans would have jobs" today and a "family of four" could expect to have "$22,776" more in their wallets.[21] Therefore, given the lessons of history that were open and obvious to Obama and his unmistakable awareness of rule of law principles and the importance of adhering to them, Obama's legacy should reflect all of the harms that naturally flow from his reckless and destructive governmental actions.

While our plight is not hopeless, it will take a rule of law renaissance to bring this country back from the arbitrary and capricious legal abyss that we are descending into. If we want to avoid becoming another Greece with rioting in the streets, it will take political leadership with the courage and wisdom of the "Iron Lady" and the American spirit and determination of a Ronald Reagan, to resuscitate the Rule of Law and our economy from the devastating challenges it presently faces.

Instead of just focusing on the constitutionality of legislation and the price tag of regulations, we should be asking whether any and all laws and regulations possess the time-tested attributes of "generality, equality of application and certainty." And if they do not, they should not become law. And if these principles become the "moral tradition of the community" in Hayek's words, the days of laws being signed by a president that are hundreds, if not thousands, of pages long that authorize hundreds of additional future regulations will be over. Few laws or regulations meet these criteria today because virtually all major pieces of legislation, which have significant economic consequences, are rife with exceptions and provisions that favor one special interest or another whether on the left or right. Our tax code is a prime example of a law that has lost its rule of law way, if it ever had one at all, in which, as we have seen, approximately 150 million people pay no federal income taxes at all and the top 3% pay more federal taxes than the other 97%.

So one might ask, where do we start to rebuild the rule of law principles into the laws of the land? There are a plethora of places to start, such as the repeal of Obama Care and starting over with health care reform that begins by reforming the wasteful medical malpractice liability system in this country which is riddled with judges abusing their discretion in the handling of tort (personal injury) cases. It has been ignored by the Obama administration largely because the trial lawyer lobby is one of the Democratic Party's major contributors. That initiative would really make a dent in the health care cost crisis in the U.S. It results in billions of wasted dollars every year - which ultimately result in higher health care insurance premiums - as doctors practice defensive medicine to protect themselves from frivolous, rule of law denigrating lawsuits filed by self-serving trial lawyers.[22]

But given America's deep-seated economic crisis, I suggest another broken piece of our legal architecture which is riddled with special interest cancer as a first step: the tax code. Enacting a flat tax into law might be the best place to begin rebuilding our respect for the Rule of Law and to lay a cornerstone for this country's economic turnaround. It would be the perfect example of a law that meets rule of law principles. With a flat rate for individuals and corporations, no individual or business is favored over another with a special provision or exemption and the "certainty" of one's tax bill - and the government's revenue stream - would become much more predictable. And there would be no need for an endless stream of new discretion laden regulations to interpret the law. Various flat tax proposals have been made by economists and political candidates over the last few decades. Whether it's Steve Forbes, Jack Kemp, Herman Cain or Newt Gingrich, there is good reason for these proposals. To date, though, its economic sense and rule of law fidelity have not been translated into the law of the land.

As the respected Reagan administration economist, Arthur Laffer, and his co-authors, Stephen Moore and Peter Tanous, point out in their thought-provoking book *The End of Prosperity*, there are basically three reasons for the current tax code: Revenue, redistribution of wealth and social engineering. They urge that we put an end to such an unproductive government policy and enact a flat tax as many countries have done already.[23] Thus, at a 15% rate, with very few deductions, the individual who makes a million dollars annually would pay $150,000 in taxes and the person who makes $100,000 would pay $15,000.

In a recent article, Laffer elaborated on why he supports a flat tax and then candidate Gingrich's tax plan, in particular. "Tax codes, in order to work well, require widespread voluntary compliance from taxpayers. And for taxpayers to voluntarily comply with a tax code, they have to believe that it is both fair and efficient. Fairness in taxation means that people and businesses in like circumstances have similar tax burdens. A flat tax, whether on businesses or individuals, achieves fairness in spades. A person who makes ten times as much as another person should pay ten times more in taxes ... The current administration's notion of fairness - taxing high income earners at high rates and not taxing other income earners at all - is totally unfair. It is also anathema to prosperity and ultimately leads to the situation we have in our nation today."

Laffer goes on to point out that Gingrich's "optional 15 % flat tax on individuals and 12.5% flat tax for business ... has been tried and tested and found enormously successful. Hong Kong, where there has been a flat tax on individuals since 1947, is truly a shining city on the hill and one of the most prosperous cities in history. Ireland's 12.5 % flat business income tax propelled the Emerald Isle out of two and a half centuries of poverty." And to answer those critics who can't get over their reliance on our failed discriminatory tax law, he says "economic growth achieved through a flat tax in conjunction with a pro-growth safety net is the only way to raise incomes of those on the bottom rungs of the economic ladder."[24]

But what economists and politicians do not seem to fully appreciate is that economically successful government policies - if they involve any form of coercion in a free society - must start with a *well designed law*—that is, one that meets the principles of the Rule of Law. (Emphasis supplied). Hayek was probably the single greatest exponent of the synergy between successful economies and the attributes of the Rule of Law. And it does not seem we could find a better example of a law that trumpets the "generality," "certainty" and "equality of application "sought by the rule of law ideal, not to mention its fairness to all concerned, than a flat tax. With a "uniform" flat tax we would truly experience a "government of laws" and not a "government of men" inasmuch as no government official is making a value judgment that "different" citizens should be treated "differently" under our laws.

Whether it involves taxes, the national debt, health care, the environment or other areas of the U.S economy, it remains to be seen how soon and to what extent the American public and their elected representatives turn away from the "welfare state" that has been creeping up on us for decades. What history shows, though, as we have seen in the pages of this book, the sooner we can reestablish the Rule of Law as "the moral tradition of the community" and limited government as our political philosophy, the sooner economic dynamism will return to our shores.

But what we do know - based on his record and personal history - is if President Obama is elected to a second term, the evidence is overwhelming that the tipping point will be reached and the Rule of Law will become unrecognizable. Then we will all be well down the "Road to Serfdom," with not much hope of finding our way home again.

END NOTES

CHAPTER 1 END NOTES

1. David Remnick, *The Bridge: The Life and Rise of Barack Obama* (New York: Alfred A. Knopf 2010), p. 187.

2. "Obama's Law," by Justin Driver, *The New Republic,* 9 June 2011, www.tnr.com/print/article/politics/magazine/89647/obama-legal-philosophy-laurence, retrieved 10/8/2011)

3. Ibid.

4. Ibid.

5. Ibid.

6. Remnick, *The Bridge*, p. 116

7. Ibid., p. 216

8. Ibid., p. 215

9. Ibid., p. 107

10. Ibid.

11. Ibid., p. 196

12. Driver, *The New Republic*, 9 June 2011.

13. Ibid.

14. Ibid.

15. Dennis Goldford, *The American Constitution and the Debate over Originalism* (Cambridge, United Kingdom: Cambridge Univ. Press 2005) p. 174.

16. "The Bork Nomination," *The Eighties Club, The Politics and Pop Culture of the 1980s*, http://eightiesclub.tripod.com id320htm

17. Ibid.

18. "Kennedy, Obama Tout Generational Change," by Bob Considine, *Today People, today.msnbc.msn.com/id/228932641/ns/today-today_peopole/t/kennedy-obama-tout-generational-change/*

19. Remnick, *The Bridge*, p. 90–92.

20. Ibid.

21. Ibid., 104.

22. Ibid., p.112.

23. Ibid., p. 118–119.

24. Barack Obama, *Dreams from My Father: A Story of Race and Inheritance* (New York: Three Rivers Press, 1995, 2004) p. 135.

25. Remnick, *The Bridge*, p. 119.

26. Ibid., p. 177.

27. "Obama's Law," by Justin Driver, *The New Republic*.

28. Remnick, *The Bridge*, p. 184.

29. Ibid.

30. Ibid., p. 183–184.

31. Ibid., p. 184.

32. Ibid., p.185; see also "Unger Leaves Harvard for Brazilian Government," by Clifford Marks, *The Harvard Crimson*, www.the crimson.com/article/2007/6/29/unger-leaves-harvard-for-brazilian-government.

33. Remnick, The Bridge, p. 184.

34. "Kagan Kicked Out Campus Recruiters at First Chance," by Ben Conery, *The Washington Times*, 12 May 2010, www.washingtontimes.com/news/…/kagan-kicked-out-campus-recruiters

35. Remnick, *The Bridge*, p. 185.

36. Ibid., pp. 191, 473.

37. "Crouching Media, Hidden racist Video," by John Hayward, *Human Events,* 3 March 2012, *http://www.humanevents.com/article.php?id=50068&keywords=john +hayward+derrick+bell*

38. "Race, Equality and the Rule of Law: Critical Race Theory's Attack on the Promise of Liberalism, by Jeffrey Pyle, *Boston College Law Review*, 1 May 1999, Vl. 40., pp. 787–827.

39. "The Skin Trade," by Richard Posner, *NEW REPUBLIC* at 40, 13 Oct.1997 (book review).

40. Remnick, *The Bridge*, p.184.

41. Ibid., p. 185.

42. Ibid., p. 184.

43. Ibid., p. 185.

44. Ibid.

45. Obama, *Dreams from My Father*, p. 437.

CHAPTER 2 END NOTES

1. F.A. Hayek, *The Constitution of Liberty* (Chicago: Univ. of Chicago Press 1960) p. 166.

2. Aristotle, Politics, Book III, 1286, p. 78.

3. Hayek, *The Constitution of Liberty*, p. 166–67.

4. Ibid., p. 172.

5. Ibid., p. 205–210.

6. Ibid.

7. Brian Tamanaha, On The Rule of Law: History, Politics, Theory (Cambridge, United kingdom: Cambridge University Press 2004) p. 124–125.

8. Ibid. p. 139.

9. "Order in the Jungle," *The Economist*, 13 May 2008.

10. John Ranelagh, Thatcher's People: An Insider's Account of the Politics, The Power, And the Personalities (Fontana, 1992), p. ix.; "Friedrich August von Hayek; Economist Influenced Reagan Policy;" Los Angeles Times, March 24, 1992, http://articles, latimes.com/1992-03-24/news/mn-4357_1_friedrich-august-von-hayek.

11. Henry Hazlitt, New York Times Book Review, *The Road To Serfdom: The Definitive Edition*, Edited by Bruce Caldwell (Chicago: The University of Chicago Press; Routledge, London, 2007 ed.) back cover.

12. Ibid., p. 31.

13. Henry Hazlitt, Newsweek, *The Constitution of Liberty* (Chicago: Univ. of Chicago Press 1960) back cover.

14. Hayek, *The Constitution of Liberty*, p. 160–161.

15. Ibid., p. 160, 208.

16. Ibid., p. 160.

17. Ibid., p. 262.

18. Ibid., p. 206.

CHAPTER 3 ENDNOTES

1. "Obama Warns Supreme Court," by Laura Meckler and Carol E. Lee, *The Wall Street Journal*, April 3, 2012, A1, A4.

2. "Contempt for the Constitution, "*The Wall Street Journal*, 13 January 2012, A12.

3. "Obama Decries Fat Cat Bankers," by Derrick Henry, *NY Times.com*, 14 December 2009, http://the caucus.blogs.nytimes.com/2009/12/14/obama-decries-fat-cat-bankers.

4. "Why Dodd-Frank Is Unconstitutional," by C. Boyden Gray and Jim R. Purcell, *The Wall Street Journal*, 22 June 2012, A 17.

5. Robert J. Barro, *Determinants of Economic Growth: A Cross Country Empirical Study* (Cambridge, Mass, London, England: The MIT Press 1997) p. 28, 35.

6. Brian Z. Tamanaha, *Law as a Means to an End* (Cambridge, United Kingdom: Cambridge University Press 2006) p. 129.

7. Brian Z. Tamanaha, *On The Rule of Law: History, Politics, Theory* (Cambridge, United Kingdom: Cambridge University Press 2004) p. 79.

8. Ibid., p. 86.

9. Pastor Rick Warren, Christmas message, Saddleback Church, Lake Forest, CA, December, 2011; Isaiah, *Life Application Study Bible: New International Version* (Wheaton, Illinois: Tyndale House Publishers, Inc. 1991) 53:6.

10. F.A. Hayek, *The Constitution of Liberty* (Chicago: Univ. of Chicago Press 1960) p. 179.

CHAPTER 4 ENDNOTES

1. "Fox Gets The Message, Calls Obama the Food Stamp President," *Media Matters*, 19 January 2012, www.mediamatters.org/research/201201190015.
2. "In Depth: Minority Unemployment in America," *CNN*, 10 August 2011, am.blogs.cnn.com/2011/08/10/in-depth-minority-unemployment-in-america.
3. "More Elderly Find They Can't Afford Not to Work," *The Wall Street Journal*, by Kelly Greene and Anne Tergesen, 21–22 January 2012, A1, A10.
4. "Obama's Keystone Delay Flouts the Law,"by Mary Anastasia O'Grady, *The Wall Street Journal*, 23 January 2012, A17.
5. Ibid.
6. "Economic Uncertainty, The Courts, And the Rule of Law," by Todd Zywicki, *Harvard Journal of Law and Public Policy*, Vl 35, Number 1, Winter 2012, pp. 202–203.
7. "Regime Uncertainty: Why The Great Depression Lasted So long and Why Prosperity Resumed After the War," by Robert Higgs, 1 *INDEP. REV.* 561, 563–64 (1997.
8. Ronald Reagan, *Ronald Reagan: The Autobiography* (New York: Simon & Schuster 1990) p. 67.
9. "Administration of Franklin D. Roosevelt: Disposition of Executive Orders Signed by Franklin D. Roosevelt," *National Archives*,http://www.archives.gov/federal-register/executive-orders/roosevelt.html
10. "List of U.S. Executive Branch Czars," *Wikipedia*, http://en.wikipedia.org/wiki/list-of-U.S.-executive-branch-czars.
11. Robert S. McElvaine, *The Great Depression* (New York: Times Books 1984) p. 307.
12. "The FDR Lesson Obama Should Follow," by Arthur Herman, *The Wall Street Journal*, 10 May 2012, A15.
13. Marion C. McKenna, *Franklin Roosevelt and the Great Constitutional War: The Court Packing Crisis of 1937* (New York: Fordham University Press 2002) p. 480–87; see also senate Committee on the Judiciary, S Rep No 711, 75th Cong., 1st sess., 1 (1937).
14. "Reorganization of the Federal Judiciary: Adverse Report from the [Senate] Committee on the Judiciary Submitted to Accompany S. 1392" (75th cong., 1st sess., Senate Report No. 711, June 7, 1937), pp. 8, 15, 20 and 19.
15. Ibid.

16. McElvaine, *The Great Depression*, p. 309.

17. "Super Switch," by Christopher Shea, *The Boston Globe*, 4 December 2005, www.boston.com/news/global/ideas/articles/2005/12/04/supreme-switch.

18. Wickard v. Filburn, 317 U.S. 111 (1942).

19. National Federation of Independent Business, et. al. v. Sebelius (Slip Opinion), No. 11-393, June 28, 2012.

20. "A Vast New Taxing Power," *The Wall Street Journal*, 2 July 2012, A 10.

CHAPTER 5 END NOTES

1. "Bill Ayres," *Wikipedia*, http://en.wikipedia.org/wiki/Bill_Ayers

2. Brian Z. Tamanaha, *On The Rule of Law: History, Politics, Theory* (Cambridge, United 3. Kingdom: Cambridge University Press 2004) p. 73.

3. Ibid., p. 74

4. Ibid.

5. David Remnick, *The Bridge: The Life and Rise of Barack Obama* (New York: Alfred A. Knopf 2010), p. 183.

6. Tamanaha, *On The Rule of Law*, p. 74.

7. Bill Scheuerman, "The Rule of Law and the Welfare State: Toward a New Synthesis," *Politics and Society*, vol 22, 22 June 1994, pp. 200–203.

8. Remnick, *The Bridge*, p. 184–185.

9. Ibid., p. 184.

10. Scheuerman, The Rule of Law and the Welfare State, p. 203, ftn 29.

11. bid.

12. Remnick, The Bridge, p. 184; see also Roberto Mangabeira Unger, *Law in Modern Society: Toward a Criticism of Social Theory* (New York: The Free Press 1976) p. 181.

13. Remnick, *The Bridge*, p. 185.

14. "Obama takes Populist Swing," by Laura Meckler, *The Wall Street Journal*, 7 December 2011, A1.

15. Unger, *Law in Modern Society*, pp. 197, 173, 181.

16. Ibid., p. 209.

17. Remnick, *The Bridge*, p. 185.

18. Unger, *Law in Modern Society*, pp. 209, 238–242.

19. "Romney made$ 42.7million in 2 years," by Jeanne Sahadi, CNN Money, 25 January 2012, http://money.cnn.com/2012/01/24/news/economy/Romney_tax_return/index.htm.

20. "Warren Buffet's Secretary Likely Makes Between $200,000 And $500,000/ Year," by Paul Roderick Gregory, Forbes, 25 January 2012, http://www.forbes.com/sites/paulrodrickgregory/2012/01/25/warren-buffets-secretary-lik...

21. Ibid.

22. "How Much the Rich Pay," *The Wall Street Journal*, 20 January 2012, A12.

23. Unger, *Law in a Modern Society*, pp. 178, 180.

24. Ibid., p. 67.

25. Ibid., p.196.

26. Ibid., p. 195.

27. Ibid., p. 198.

28. "The Loan Quota Rule," *The Wall Street Journal*, 27 January 2012, A14.

29. Unger, *Law in Modern Society*, p. 198.

30. "Obama critic so far left he's no help to the right," by Margery Eagan, *Boston Herald* .com, 19 June2012, www. BostonHerald.com/news/columnists/view/2022061obama_critic_far_left_h...

31. Tamanaha, *Law as a Means to an End*, p. 151.

32. Ibid., p. 153; see also Laurence Solum, "2005 Entry Level Hiring Report," 26 April 2005, *Legal Theory Blog*.

33. Tamanaha, *Law as a Means to an End*, p. 150.

34. Richard Tarnas, *The Passion of the Western Mind: Understanding the Ideas that have Shaped our World View* (New York: Harmony Books 1991); see also *Law as a Means to an End*, p. 113.

CHAPTER 6 END NOTES

1. Theodore M. Hesburgh with Jerry Reedy, *God, Country, Notre Dame: The Autobiography of Theodore M. Hesburgh* (New York: Doubleday 1990), p. 303.

2. Rick Perlstein, Nixonland: The Rise of a President and the Fracturing of America (Simon and Schuster 2008), pp. 383, 420

3. Hesburgh, *God, Country, Notre Dame*, p. 66.

4. Ibid., p. 106.

5. Ibid., pp. 95–103; 190, 208.

6. Ibid., p. 108.

7. Ibid., pp. 109–110.

8. Ibid., p. 112.

9. Ibid., p. 113.

10. Ibid., p. 115.

11. Ibid., pp. 1116–118.

12. Ibid., pp. 126–128.

13. Ibid., pp. 116–117.

CHAPTER 7 ENDNOTES

1. Jim Newton, *Justice For All: Earl Warren and the Nation He Made* (New York, New York, Riverhead Books, Penguin Group, 2006) p. 10–11

2. Ibid., p. 5

3. Ibid., p. 483

4. Brian Z. Tamanaha, *Law as a Means to an End* (Cambridge, United Kingdom: Cambridge University Press 2006) p. 86.

5. Ibid., p. 97.

6. Ronald Reagan, *An American Life: The Autobiography* (New York, New York: Simon and Schuster 1990) pp. 279–280).

7. Newton, *Justice For All*, p. 10.

8. Ibid., p. 69.

9. Ibid., p. 394.; see also *Engel v. Vitale*, 370 U.S. 421 (1962).

10. Tamanaha, *Law as a Means to an End*, p.65, 86.

11. Ibid., p. 65; see also *Kingsley Int Pictures v Regents* (1959) and *Griswold v. Connecticut*, 381 U.S. 479 (1965).

12. *Miranda*, 384 U.S. 436 (1966).

13. *Shapiro v. Thompson* 394 U.S. 618 (1969); see also Tamanaha, *Law as a Means to an End*, p. 87.

14. *Roe v. Wade*, 410 U.S. 113 (1973); see also Newton, *Justice For All*, p. 455.

15. Newton, *Justice For All*, p. 455.

16. *Roe v. Wade* 410 U.S. 113 (1973).

17. Tamanaha, *Law as a means to an End*, p. 88–89.

18. Ibid., p. 97.

19. "The Obama Care Recusal Nonsense," by Michael Mukasey, *Wall Street Journal*, 5 December 2011, A17.

20. "Leaked: Obama Mentor's Blunt Advice on Court Choices," *The Caucus, The Politics and Government blog of The New York Times*, 28 October 2010, http://thecaucus.blogs.nytimes.com/2010/10/28/leaked-obama-mentors-blunt-advice-on-court-choices/

21. Letter from Laurence H. Tribe, Carl M. Loeb University Professor, Harvard University, to President Obama, 4 May 2009; see also "Obama's Law," by Justin Driver, *The New Republic*, 9 June 2011,www.tnr.com/print/article/politics/magazine/89647/ obama-legal-philosophy-laurence…

22. Ibid.

23. Ibid.
24. Ibid.
25. "Obama Pushes for Empathetic Supreme Court Justices," *Fox News.com,* 1 May 2009, http://www.foxnews.com/politics/2009/05/01/obama-pushes-empathetic-supreme-court-justices/
26. Tribe Letter to Obama, May 4, 2009.
27. Ibid.
28. Ibid.
29. Antonin Scalia, *A Matter of Interpretation: Federal Courts and The Law* (Princeton, New Jersey; Princeton Univ. Press 1997) pp. 24–25.
30. Stephen Breyer, *Active Liberty, Interpreting Our Democratic Constitution* (New York: Knopf, 2005) p. 111.
31. *National Federation of Independent Business, et al v. Sebelius* (Slip Opinion), No. 11-393, June 28, 2012.
32. Breyer, *Active Liberty*, p. 18.
33. Ibid., pp. 129, 119.
34. Ibid., p. 119.
35. Madison, Hamilton and Jay, *The Federalist Papers,* No. 78, p. 478.
36. *Osborn v. Bank of United States*, 22 US (9 Wheaton) 736, 866 (1824).
37. Friedrich Hayek, *The Constitution of Liberty* (Chicago,: Univ. of Chicago Press 1960) p. 153.
38. Brian Tamanaha, *On The Rule of Law: History, Politics, Theory* (Cambridge, United Kingdom: Cambridge Univ. Press 2004) p. 124.
39. "A Dissection of the Obama Care Ruling," by John Eastman, *Right Reason, Center for Jurisprudence and Natural Law, The Claremont Institute*, 28 June 2012, http://www.right-reason.org/publications/pubid.802/pub_detail.asp
40. "A Vast New Taxing Power," *The Wall Street Journal*, 2 July 2012, A 10.
41. Transcript of Alito Opening Statement before Senate Judiciary Committee, *The New York Times*, 10 January 2006, A18.

CHAPTER 8 END NOTES

1. "Spread the Wealth," by Natalie Gewargis, *Political Punch, ABC News Blogs*, 14 October 2008, ABC News. Com, http://abcnews.go.com/blogs/politics/2008/10/spread-the-weal/
2. "45% of U.S. Households Paid no Federal Tax," by Kay Bell, *MSN Money*, 25 April 2011, http://money.msn.com/tax-tips/post.aspx?post=292d620a-6459-4381-a22b-f3b59dc64ff8

End Notes

3. Bill Scheuerman, "The Rule of law and the Welfare State; Toward a New Synthesis," 22 *Politics and Society* 195 (June 1994).

4. "January Jobs Report: Hiring Ramps Up, Unemployment Falls," by Annalyn Censky, *CNN Money*, 3 February 2012, http://money.cnn.com/2012/02/03/ news/economy/jobs_ report unemployment/index.htm;

5. "Half of U.S. Mortgages are Effectively Under Water," by Diana Olick, *CNBC*, 8 November 2011, http://www.cnbc.com/id/45209336/half of US Mortgages_Are_Effectively_Underwater.

6. Friedrich Hayek, *The Constitution of Liberty* (Chicago: The Univ. of Chicago Press 1960) p. 88.

7. Ibid., p. 93.

8. John Ranelagh, Thatcher's People: An Insider's Account of the Politics, The Power, And the Personalities (London: Harper Collins Publishers (1991), pp. 8–9.

9. "100 Years of the American Economic Review: The Top 20 Articles," by Kenneth Arrow, B. Douglas Bernheim, Daniel L. Mc Fadden, James M. Poterba, and Robert M. Solow, *American Economic Review*, 2011, 101(1).

10. "The Use of knowledge in Society," by F.A. Hayek, The *American Economic Review*, September, 1945, pp. 519–530.

11. Ranelagh, *Thatcher's People*, p. 189.

12. Alan O. Ebenstein, *Friedrich Hayek: A Biography* (Chicago: Univ. of Chicago Press 2003) p. 305.

13. Ranelagh, *Thatcher's People*, p. ix.

I14. Ibid., p. 189.

15. John Blundell, *Margaret Thatcher: A portrait of the Iron Lady* (Algora 2008) ISBN978-0-87586-630-7, pp.25–26; Andy Beckett, *When the lights Went Out: Britain in the Seventies* (Faber & Faber 2010) ISBN 978-0-571-22137-0, p.25.

16. Ranelagh, *Thatcher's People*, p. 193.

17. "Economic Uncertainty, The Courts, And the Rule of Law," by Todd Zywicki, *Harvard Journal of Law and Public Policy*, Vl 35, Number 1, Winter 2012, pp. 196-197; see also F.A. Hayek, "The Use of Knowledge in Society" 35 AM. ECON. REV. 519, 526-27 (1945); F.A. Hayek, Law Legislation and Liberty (3rd prtg. 1998), pp. 108–09.

18. "The 100 Best Non-Fiction Books of the Century," *National Review*, www.nationalreview.com/100 best// 100_books.html.)

19. "Economics for the Long Run," by John Taylor, *the Wall Street Journal*, 25 January 2012, A17.

20. Martin Anderson, *Revolution* (Harcourt Brace Jovanovich 1988) p. 164.

21. George H. W. Bush, Remarks on Presenting the Presidential Medal of Freedom Awards, 18 November 1991.

22. F.A. Hayek, *The Road to Serfdom* (Chicago: University of Chicago Press 2007 [1944]) p. 113.

23. "Boeing, Machinists Union Reach Tentative Deal to Settle NLRB Dispute," by Amy Bingham, *ABC News, The Note*, 1 December 2011 http://abcnews.go.com/blogs/politics/2011/12/boeing-machinist-union-reach-tentative-deal-to-settle-nlrb-dispute/

24. Hayek, *The Road to Serfdom*, pp. 112-114.

25. Ibid., p. 96.

26. F.A. Hayek, "Preface 1976" in *The Road To Serfdom* (Chicago: Univ. of Chicago Press 2007 [1944]) pp. 54–55.

27. Sonia Orwell and Ian Angus (eds.), *The Collected Essays, Journalism and Letters of George Orwell* (London: Penguin, 1970), Vol . 3, p. 143.; see also Ranelagh, Thatcher's People, p. 192.

28. "Opinion," *The Wall Street Journal*, 15 December 2011.

29. Roberto Mangabeira Unger, *Law in Modern Society: Toward a Criticism of Social Theory* (New York: The Free Press 1976) p. 198

30. Ibid.

31. "What Would The Iron Lady Do?" By Charles Moore, *The Wall Street Journal*, 17-18 December 2011, C1-2.

32. Margaret Thatcher, *The Path To Power* (New York: Harper Collins 1995) p.p. 50–51; see also "Thatcher Offers Clues to Economic Resurgence," by George Ball, *The Orange County Register*, 4 May 2011, http://www.ocregister.com/articles/government-299127-britain-economic.html

33. Jose Harris, "Beveridge's Social and Political Thought," *Beveridge and Social Security, An International Retrospective,* ed. by John Hills, John Ditch and Howard Glennerster, (Oxford: Clarendon Press 1994); see also Hayek, *The Road To Serfdom* Introduction (2007) ed. by Bruce Caldwell, p. 14, ftn. 45.

34. Thatcher, *The Path to Power*, p. 572; see also "U.S. Deficit at 1.3 trillion in Fiscal 2011,"*Reuters*, 7 October 2011, www.reuters.com/article/2011/10/07/U.S>/USA-debt-cbo-idustre79651A20111007.

35. "Margaret Thatcher: The Debt We Still Owe Her," *Mail Online*, 4/25/08, www.dailymail.co.uk/debate/columnists/article/562178/margaret-Thatcher-the-debt…

36. Thatcher, *The Path To Power*, p. 50.

37. Ibid., pp. 50–51

38. Ibid., p. 85.

39. Ibid., p. 84

40. Ibid., pp. 50–51.

41. Margaret Thatcher, *The Downing Street Years* (New York: Harper Collins 1993) p. 6.

42. Thatcher, *The Path To Power*, p. 313.

43. Thatcher, *The Downing Street Years,* pp. 6–7.

44. Thatcher, *Path to Power*, p. 567.

45. Ibid., p. 31.

46. Ibid., p. 40

47. Ibid., pp. 439–440.

48. "What Would the Iron Lady Do?" By Charles Moore, *The Wall Street Journal*, 17–18 December 2011, C1-2.

49. Thatcher, *The Path to Power*, pp. 570–78.

50. YOU TUBE, www.Youtube .com/watch?v=okHGCz6xxiw.

CHAPTER 9 END NOTES

1. Richard Hofstadter, *The American Political Tradition: And The Men Who Made It* (New York: Vintage 1989 [1948]) p. xxxvii; see also Brian Tamanaha, *Law As A Means To An End* (New York: Cambridge Univ. Press 2006) pp. 37–38.

2. "$ 5 Trillion and Change," *The Wall Street Journal*, 1 February 2012, A 14.

3. Robert Barro, *Determinants of Economic Growth: A Cross- Country Empirical Study* (Cambridge, Mass., The MIT Press 1997), pp. 119, 26, 28.

4. "2012 Index of Economic Freedom," *The Heritage Foundation*, http://www. heritage.org/index/book/executive-highlights

5. "A Step Backward for Economic Freedom in 2012," by Edward J. Fuelner, *The Wall Street Journal*, http://online.wsj.com/article/SB100014240529702042 5750457715124184733554.html)

6. "The Jobs Rally," *The Wall Street Journal*, 10-11 March 2012, A12.

7. "Economic Uncertainty, The Courts, And the Rule of Law," by Todd Zywicki, *Harvard Journal of Law and Public Policy*, Vl 35, Number 1, Winter 2012, pp. 206–207.)

8. Ibid., p. 195.

9. Ibid., pp. 202–203.

10. "Buffet Rule: Not Ready for prime time," by Jeanne Sahadi, CNN Money, 15 February 2012, http://money.cnn.com/2012/02/15/news/economy/Obama_ Buffett_taxes/index.htm;

11. "Chart of the Week: Nearly Half of All Americans Don't Pay income Taxes," *The Foundry, The Heritage Network*, by Rob Bluey, 19 February 2012, http://blog.heritage.org/2012/02/19/chart-of-the-week-nearly-half-of-all-americans-dont-pay-income-taxes/

12. "Obama's Dividend Assault," The Wall Street Journal, 22 February 2012, A14; see also "Comparing the Candidates Tax Plans," *The Wall Street Journal*, 23 February 2012, A4.

13. Ibid; see also "The Amazing Obama budget," *The Wall Street Journal,* 14 February 2012, A18.

14. "Supreme Court's Health Care Ruling Dominates Debate, Shapes Election," by Christina Bellatoni and Terence Burlij, *PBS News Hour, The Rundown-The Morning Line,* 2 July 2012, http://www.pbs.org/newshour/rundown/2012/07/court-ruling-dominates-debate-shapes-election.html

15. "Mortgage Settlement Or Mortgage Shakedown?" by David Skeel, *The Wall Street Journal*, 21 February 2012, A 19.

16. "Obama seeks to double auto fuel economy by 2025" by Wendy Koch, USA Today.com, 16 November 2011, http://content.usatoday.com/communities/greenhouse/post/2011/11/obama-seeks-to-doubl…)

17. Ibid.

18. "Obama's CAFÉ Fuel Economy Standards To Create Fleet of Tiny, Expensive Vehicles," by Multiple Authors, *Car and Driver*, May, 2009, http://www.caranddriver.com/news/obamas-cafe-fuel-economy-standards-to-create-fleet-of-tiny-expensive-vehicles-car-news.

19. "Automobile Fuel Economy Standards," by Sam Kazman, *The Competitive Enterprise Institute,* http://cei.org/cei_files/fm/active/0/EnvironmentalSource_EnergyAuto.pdf)

20. "Why The Government's CAFÉ Standards for Fuel Efficiency Should Be Repealed, not Increased," by Charli Coon, 11 July 2001, http://www.heritage.org/research/reports/2001/07/cafe-standards -should-be-repealed; see also "Auto CAFE Standards: Unsafe and Unwise at Any Level," by William Laffler III, 19 April 1991, www. Heritage.org/research/reports/1991/04/bbg825-auto-café-standards-unsafe-and-u)

21. "Obama's Decision on Contraceptives Won't Stop Legislative Push," by Alex M. Parker, U.S. News, http://www.usnews.com/news/articles/2012/02/10/obama-decision-on-contraceptives-wont-stop-legislative-push

22. "A Message from Father John Jenkins, CSC, President, University of Notre Dame," May 21, 2012, email message of May 21, 2012 from the Office of the President to the Notre Dame community.

23. "The Avastin Denial," *The Wall Street Journal*, 19-20 November 2011, A 14.

24. "Crucify Them," *The Wall Street Journal*, 27 April 2012, A 14.

25. "Morning Bell: Tangled Up in Washington's Red Tape," by Mike Brownfield, *The Foundry, The Heritage Network*, 27 July 2011.)

26. "Over-regulated America," *The Economist,* Vl 402, Number 8772, 18 February 2012, p. 9.

CHAPTER 10 END NOTES

1. Roberto Mangabeira Unger, *Law in Modern Society: Toward a Criticism of Social Theory* (New York: The Free Press 1976) p. 64–67, 51–54.

2. "DNC Playing a role in Wisconsin Protests," by Ben Smith, *POLITCO, http:// www.politico.com/blogs/bensmith/0211/DNC_playing_role_in_Wisconsin_protests. html?showall*

3. "Real Lesson of Cambridge Moment Is injustice of Misapplied Empathy," by George Ball, *Investor's Business* Daily, 31 July 2009, A11.

4. "President Obama Says Arizona's Poorly Conceived Immigration Law could Mean Hispanic Americans are Harassed," ABC News, by Kristina Wong, 27 April 2010, http://abcnews.go.com/blogs/politics/2010/04/president-obama-says-arizonas-poorlyconceived-immigration-law-could-mean-hispanicamericans-are-haras/

5. Arizona v. United States, Slip Opinion, No. 11-182, June 25, 2012.

6. "Obama to Halt Deportation of Undocumented immigrants Without Criminal Records, *Fox News*, 18 August 2011, http://latino.foxnews.com/latino/ politics/2011/08/18/obama-to-halt-deportation-undocumented-immigrants-without-criminal-records/

7. "Obama to stop deporting some young illegal immigrants," by Tom Cohen, *CNN*, 16 June 2012http://www.cnn.com/2012/06/15/politics/immigration/ index.html

8. David Remnick, *The Bridge: The Life and Rise of Barack Obama* (New York: Alfred A. Knopf 2010), p. 184.

9. Barack Obama, *Audacity of Hope: Thoughts on Reclaiming the American Dream* (New York, Crown Publishers 2006), p. 87.

10. Ibid., p. 84.

11. Ibid., 267.

12. "Recap: Supreme Court Live Blog: The Immigration Case," *Washington Wire, The Wall Street Journal*, http://blogs.wsj.com/washwire/2012/04/25/ supreme-court-live-blog-the-immigration-case/

13. "Wallace let's McConnell criticize reconciliation even though he previously supported it,", *Media Matters*, 21 February 2010, http://mediamatters.org/video/2010/02/21/wallace-lets-mcconnell-criticize-reconciliation/160709

14. "Ration Trial Lawyers, Not Services to Lower the Cost of Health Care," by George Ball, 7 July 2009, *Investor's Business Daily*, A 13; "The Real Lesson of Cambridge Moment is the injustice of Misapplied Empathy," by George Ball, *Investor's Business Daily* 31 July 2009, A 11.

15. "The Supreme Court and Congress: What Happens in Congress After The Supreme Court Strikes Down Legislation," by J Mitchell Pickerell, *Insights on Law & Society*, *The American Bar Association*, Fall 2006, 7.1.

16. Friedrich Hayek, *The Constitution of Liberty* (Chicago,: Univ. of Chicago Press 1960) p. 153.

17. *Osborn v. Bank of United States*, 22 US (9 Wheaton) 736, 866 (1824).

18. Antonin Scalia, *A Matter of Interpretation: Federal Courts and The Law (Princeton*, New Jersey; Princeton Univ. Press 1997) pp. 24–25.

19. "Averting Obama Court is Now A Priority," by George Ball, *Investor's Business Daily*, 22 December 2009, A 13.

20. Brian Z. Tamanaha, *Law as a Means to an End* (Cambridge, United Kingdom: Cambridge University Press 2006) p. 174.

21. "The Financial Recession Excuse," by Phil Gramm and Mike Solon, *The Wall Street Journal*, 2 February 2012, A13.

22. "Ration Trial Lawyers, Not Services, To Lower The Cost Of Health Care," by George Ball, *Investor's Business Daily*, 7 July 2009, A 13.

23. Arthur Laffer, Stephen Moore and Peter Tanous, *The End of Prosperity* (New York, Threshold Editions 2008), pp. 239–59.

24. "Why Gingrich's Tax Plan Beats Romney's," *The Wall Street Journal*, 31 January 2012, A 15.

17522259R00072

Made in the USA
Lexington, KY
13 September 2012